"Leadership releases people... When I reviewed Carl George's new book, I shouted to myself, 'This is what we've been looking for!' I've already decided to buy them in quantity and use them as our primary training tool for our Grace Group ministry."

Gary D. Kinnaman, Senior Pastor, Word of Grace Church, Mesa, Arizona

"When Carl George writes a book, I read it. This one is no exception... This book shows you how to develop empowered leaders and small groups that multiply – and minimize failures."

Bill Easum, Executive Director, 21st Century Strategies, Port Arkansas, Texas

"Carl George knows the power of a church when the people are put to work. This book shows how to put that power to work in your church."

Elmer L. Towns, Dean, School of Religion, Liberty University, Lynchburg, Virginia

*"The landscape in which the church carries out its mission increasingly resembles the Apostolic era. Every congregation, whether it knows it or not, is now a frontline missionary training and staging center. Models for **being** the church and raising up **leaders** within the church are desperately needed."*
"Carl George has done it! With words written not for speculation but for action, he has put into the hand of every growing believer in Christ a practical and Biblical game plan."
"God will use this tool to grow His kingdom and make an eternal difference in countless lives!"

John Messmann, Senior Pastor, St. Paul Lutheran Church, Fort Worth, Texas

"A practical, readable, down-to-earth book that will give small group leaders foundational keys to empower them for an effective, life-changing ministry."

Colin Noyes, Director, Direction Ministry Resources, Queensland, Australia

"Finally, a map through the small-group maze that offers not just hope, but concrete help! The aim is singular: the people of God equipped and set loose for ministry. A must-read for 21st-century church leaders!"

Michael W. Foss, Senior Pastor, Prince of Peace Lutheran Church, Burnsville, Minnesota

i

"We are ecstatic about this book! It has clear, workable answers to the most difficult discipling problems."

Laurel Buckingham, Senior Pastor, Wesleyan Church, Moncton, New Brunswick, Canada

"Once again Carl George prepares the pathway to effective, God-honoring, lay-empowering ministry, with clarity and insight."

G. John Baergen, Executive Director, International Centre for Leadership Development and Evangelism, Kelowna, British Columbia, Canada

"We are praying to see thousands of new missionary churches begun in the coming decade, to share in a great harvest in North America. Without healthy and effective group leadership, this cannot happen. We rejoice that Carl George's new book addresses this need and we joyfully recommend it to all our missionary supporters."

Jon C. Schuler, General Secretary, North American Mission Society, Pawleys Island, South Carolina

"Must reading for every small-group leader and church staff member. My only regret is that it wasn't written sooner."

Randy Pope, Senior Pastor, Perimeter Church, Duluth, Georgia

"Carl George has provided a desperately needed resource on leadership among the people of God. Our church has had Carl with us, weighed his counsel seriously, and applied it with great effectiveness."

Rubel Shelly, Senior Minister, Woodmont Hills Church of Christ, Nashville, Tennessee

"Carl George is a good friend and trusted advisor to First United Methodist Church in Houston. His new book, based on the truths of the Scripture, will impact your ministry in a new and exciting way."

William Hinson, Senior Pastor, First United Methodist Church, Houston, Texas

*"The practical principles in **Nine Keys** help any leader unlock the door to greater effectiveness in Kingdom work."*

Karen Hurston, Hurston Ministries and Consultation Service, Gulf Breeze, Florida

"Carl George's best yet! A refreshingly clear, practical guide to developing the life and witness of small groups, governed by agape love, and the equipping of both the existing and the new generation of small-group leaders."

John Mallison, Founder, Australian Small Group Network

Nine Keys

to Effective Small Group Leadership

How lay leaders can establish dynamic and healthy cells, classes, or teams

Carl F. George with Warren Bird

Foreword by
Robert E. Coleman

Kingdom™
publishing
Mansfield, PA

Printed in the United States of America.

Kingdom, Publishing   phone: 800-597-1123
Lambs Creek Road   phone: 717-662-7515
P.O. Box 486   fax: 717-662-3875
Mansfield, PA 16933   Internet: http://www.kingdom.com/

ISBN number: 1-883906-13-X
Library of Congress Catalog Card number: 97-72776

WHY READ THIS BOOK?

As a person who has coached small group leaders, I have searched extensively for training materials. I have yet to locate anything comparable to what you are about to read.

Carl George has tremendous insight into what actually works in small groups. In my own personal use of the leadership perspectives he describes, I've seen dramatic impact for the kingdom of God. You, too, can benefit from his expertise.

After 16 years as a pastor, Carl George was called from his local church ministry in 1978 to begin mobilizing other churches. Numerous teams of pastors and their staffs urged Carl to share his insights across the church. Since then, Carl has become one of the nation's foremost church consultants. Carl has advised some of North America's most recognized leaders! He is respected internationally by leaders in churches large and small. He is the author of many books and learning materials that impact the direction of countless congregations around the nation and the world.

Carl's extensive observations, coupled with his research findings, convinced him that God is leading many churches into a quiet revolution. It is a revolution in which lay leaders become ministry partners with their pastors. This insight prompted him to devote years of study and testing to learn what is required to enable small group leaders to be effective. He has identified key factors which work in all sizes of churches across the continent and in all major denominations and worship traditions.

As new publishers, we can introduce few authors of our generation who are as qualified to write what we hope will become the definitive text on small groups for the coming years.

In His Service,

Rachael N. Berguson
Rachael N. Berguson
Director, Kingdom Publishing

P.S.   I urge you to spend time seeking God in prayer as you begin to absorb these principles. This book will help you influence lives for eternity.

CONTENTS

FOREWORD

I have heard it said that Carl George is ahead of his time in the way he envisions church health and growth through small-group multiplication. The truth is, however, that he is only calling us back to the world's oldest, most elemental pattern of spiritual formation.

The idea goes back to the Garden of Eden when God created a family and ordained that the home become the center for procreation of the human race. Lest we miss the explosive power of a few kindred hearts knit together in love, God had the principle written in the Law given to Moses (see Deuteronomy 6:6-9).

Jesus brings the model beautifully into focus in His selection of the Twelve. While ministering to the multitudes, He developed close relationships with a few disciples. Together they learned what it meant to seek first the kingdom, and teach others to do the same. This way of life was finally bequeathed to His followers in the Great Commission (see Matthew 28:19-20).

After Pentecost, the apostolic church continued the practice of meeting in groups for "devoting themselves to the apostles' teaching and to fellowship, to the breaking of bread and to prayer" (Acts 2:42 NASB). Such family-like discipline in some way has characterized vital discipleship in the Body of Christ throughout history, especially in periods of great spiritual renewal.

It is encouraging to see a resurgence of this pattern today. Many in the organized church are tired of merely going through perfunctory motions of religion. They want something more satisfying–a relationship that is real with God and with fellow believers. If only they could come into a community of like-minded souls where the love of Christ is felt and expressed!

It is also apparent today that persons outside the church are becoming unimpressed with traditional impersonal ways of getting their attention. Lifeless, stereotyped programs of evangelism bore them. To reach these disinterested worldlings, more relational approaches must be found.

...many groups presently functioning through the church are ingrown and lethargic, with no winsome witness beyond themselves.

Invigorated small-group activity is one answer. Unfortunately, though, I am afraid many groups presently functioning through the church are ingrown and lethargic, with no winsome witness beyond themselves. Making matters worse, too often leaders in these groups do not know how to change things.

This book speaks to our need for practical leadership training. With profound simplicity, it describes how groups grow through loving relationships as you build up one another in the faith. More importantly, you learn ways to prepare yourself for leadership in the group. The sequential steps show you how to bring others into the circle of love, and in the process, how to enlarge your outreach by multiplying disciplemakers.

It is this last emphasis that distinguishes the book and sets it apart from most of the literature in the field. You may be sure, too, that however you may serve as a leader, the principles enumerated here apply to your ministry.

What gives the account authenticity is the author's own experiences of leadership. As few men of our generation, Carl George has led leaders to discover the potential of their small-group ministry. To many he has opened a whole new perspective on church health and vitality.

If what he advocates is ahead of the programs in some institutional churches, it is time for us to catch up and join ranks. Confident that the counsel in this book can help us all more effectively fulfill Christ's calling to make disciples, I joyfully commend it to you.

Robert E. Coleman, Ph.D.
Deerfield, Illinois

Dr. Coleman is Director of the School of World Mission and Evangelism and Professor of Evangelism at Trinity International University in Deerfield, Illinois. He also serves as Director of the Billy Graham Institute at Wheaton, Illinois, and Dean of the International Schools of Evangelism. Twenty-one books have come from his pen, including The Master Plan of Evangelism. *Translations of one or more of his books are published in 90 languages, with English editions alone having a combined circulation of about 5,000,000 copies.*

ACKNOWLEDGMENTS

This book would not be possible without the contributions of numerous special people. The following words of acknowledgment represent but a small token of my appreciation for your contribution to my life and learnings.

To my family, Grace George, my aptly named partner in marriage and life for 34 years, our six children, and our two grandchildren.

To my colleague, Warren Bird, who has served as editor on most of my published work. Over the years we have worked together, he has demonstrated qualities of loyalty and integrity that exceed his formidable skills in organizing and clarifying. Much of the blessing that comes to my readers would not be possible were it not for Warren's diligence and commitment to bring help to church leaders. I thank God for an editor who has demonstrated qualities of intellect, Christian compassion, and perseverance that multiply my ministry many times over. I am grateful to count him a dear and trusted friend.

To many friends, small group leaders, and ministry colleagues who contributed to the shaping of the manuscript, from transcribing cassettes to making valuable editorial suggestions: Lamar Austin, Karan Banando, John Baergen, Lorraine Baergen, Tim Barnes, David Bartels, Shelley Bartels, Juanita Berguson, Johnny Berguson, Gretchen Bird, Michelle Bird, Nathan Bird, Loren Brubaker, Tom Clegg, Roger Cutler, Jan Dale, Robert Damon, Mark Edwards, Jason Fry, Julie Gorman, Kenny Grindall, Bruce Hansen, Dave Hricik, James Hobby, Steve Maurer, Pat McGlade, Alan McMahan, John Messmann, Pat Springle, Jonathan Schaeffer, Gwen Weaver, Ron Woodworth, and Ben Zabriskie.

To churches and pastors who hosted seminars or training, or who participated in interviews that contributed to the distilling of this book. Field sites include:

- Atlanta Metropolitan Church; Atlanta, Georgia
- Bethesda Christian Church; Detroit, Michigan
- Centre Street Evangelical Church; Calgary, Alberta
- The Coastlands, Aptos Foursquare Church; Aptos, California
- First Baptist Church; Pomona, California
- First United Methodist Church; Houston, Texas
- Gateway Cathedral; Staten Island, New York
- Ginghamsburg United Methodist Church; Tipp City, Ohio
- House of the Lord; Akron, Ohio
- Metro Church; Edmond, Oklahoma
- Mississauga Gospel Temple; Mississauga, Ontario
- Sherwood Park Alliance Church; Sherwood Park, Alberta
- St. Paul Lutheran Church; Fort Worth, Texas
- Trinity Baptist Church; Kelowna, British Columbia
- Trinity Lutheran Church; Lisle, Illinois
- West Meadows Baptist Church; Edmonton, Alberta
- Word of Grace Church; Mesa, Arizona
- WSFJ-TV 51; Columbus, Ohio

Finally, to the literally hundreds of thousands of **small group leaders across the continent**: May God use you to change the way church is done in North America. Because of God's work through you, may the twenty-first century church be filled with the kind of small groups where people can see and meet Christ, and experience significant life changes.

PART 1

INTRODUCTION TO PART 1

WOULD YOU LIKE TO PLAY A PART IN MAKING YOUR CHURCH A body where significant life-changing events can occur regularly? Every congregation, including yours, already has the necessary ingredients, especially in your small groups of people who meet in the name of Jesus Christ within a context that encourages ministry one to another—and to others beyond the group.

I am convinced that effective small-group ministry must accomplish three goals:
• Provide nurturing relationships in the presence of Jesus Christ.
• Invite others to faith in Jesus Christ.
• Reproduce a new set of leaders so new groups can be formed.

Most small-group ministries accomplish the *first* objective. It's exciting to realize that every time a group convenes in Jesus' name, it becomes a place where Christ shows up and ministers through His body.

The *second* objective is met spontaneously in about one-fourth of the cases I've encountered. My prayer is that by acting more intentionally, this evangelism rate will be doubled so that at least half of North America's small groups will see conversion growth during the course of any 12-month period.

The *third* objective is approached haphazardly in most churches. In

1

reality, perhaps the most strategic thing a church's leadership can do is to help raise up another generation of leaders. They, in turn, will make the growth of even more small groups possible.

This book, therefore, has a twofold objective: helping small groups produce both new believers *and* new leaders. If you want to see more people come to Christ, you must create more places where people can see and meet Christ. If you want to multiply the number of people becoming disciples of Jesus Christ, you have to multiply the number of disciplemakers.

Is your small group (class, team, commission, cell, circle, Bible study, or whatever you call it) a birthing ward ready for new arrivals? Is it a "safe house" marked by healthy family relationships of listening and care? Is it a launch pad for mobilizing spiritual gifts? Is it a garden for growing new leaders?

The invitation and vision of this book are for you to help form the kind of church where dramatic life transformation happens routinely—hungry souls are pouring in; people are finding meaningful relationships; men, women, and children are coming to faith in Christ; believers are maturing into fully committed followers of Jesus Christ; and new leaders are constantly released for ministry, all in the context of Biblical community. That's the game plan for twenty-first century ministry.

Let's seize the opportunity before us!

CHAPTER 1

YOU ARE A WINDOW INFLUENCING SOMEONE'S ETERNITY

NOT TOO LONG AGO A PASTOR PHONED ME, SO EXCITED THAT he could barely talk. "We had something happen in one of our small groups that you *must* hear about," he enthused. Without waiting for my response, he continued to relate this story:

For the last nine months, a business owner had been attending one of their church's small groups. The previous week this man had called his group leader and announced, "I would like to say a word to the group tonight. Could you please save me some time?"

The evening's meeting was to be an unstructured potluck meal. Every so often the group ate together in place of its regular focus.

The leader, finding this request a bit formal, said, "Well of course, but you know you're always welcome to say something to us."

"No, tonight is special," replied the businessman. "I want you to be sure to set aside a few minutes for me."

The members gathered as planned, enjoying fun and fellowship over supper. Then the leader called on the man.

"There's something I need to tell you," the man began. "This week I

3

discovered that I really need to know God. So I thought, 'If I'm going to make a major religious decision, I need to do it with my family present.' Then I realized that when it comes to spiritual matters, *you* are my family. No one is as close to me or as good to me in all I've been through as I've tried to find God. So if I'm going to have my family present when I respond to God, then I need to do it here with you."

The room had become silent by this point. Tears began to well up in the eyes of several men and women who had been praying over the weeks for a spiritual breakthrough in the life of their new friend.

After a pause, the businessman continued. "What I'd like to know is this: If I'm ready to accept the Lord Jesus as my Savior, would it be okay if I did it right here in our group? Would you help me pray now, tonight?"

He bowed his head and the others present did likewise. They prayed together as he received Christ in the presence of his spiritual family.

"If I'm ready to accept the Lord Jesus as my Savior, would it be okay if I did it right here in our group?"

What a magnificent example of God's marvelous work through a healthy small group! What a tremendous encouragement to everyone from the angels in heaven to the entire church!

Another pastor told me a similar story, but this minister's tone conveyed a sense of discomfort. "As you know," he began when he saw me at a seminar, "if you're not born into our church, the proper starting point is to attend worship services for awhile. Then each quarter you have opportunity to enroll in the pastor's class. At Lesson Four we invite you to make a confession of faith, if you're not a professing Christian. Then, as appropriate, we take you through baptism and membership in a prescribed, orderly way."

Then he gave a nervous sort of chuckle. "In recent years, we've tried to create a more comprehensive care system for our people, so we launched a number of home Bible studies. It didn't occur to us that they might invite non-Christians to their meetings, so we didn't give them any instructions about how to handle outsiders."

I could tell this story had a surprise ahead!

"We have a case where someone invited one of his friends to attend their group. That friend now claims to have put his trust in Christ at one of their meetings."

Then came the clincher: "This new convert is not a standard-process person," said the pastor giving me this account. "What am I going to do with him?"

Before I could say anything in response, he broke into a grin, explaining that he was speaking tongue-in-cheek, trying to pull my leg. Not only was the story true, he said, but it represented a significant shift. For the first time in the history of their church, the pastor's class was no longer the primary avenue through which people were making professions of faith. "I don't know if everybody in our denomination can handle what's happening," he concluded, "but it certainly seems consistent with the kinds of things the Holy Spirit did in the book of Acts."

Something New in the Wind?

I enjoy hearing exciting stories like these. I have studied church health and evangelism as a full-time occupation for almost two decades, and am convinced that these "side-door" conversion experiences are increasing in number.

The Holy Spirit is doing something profound, powerful, and important. Christ's followers, through the various social units that are part of any local church, are expressing the message of Christ to people they've loved, accepted, comforted, served, and prayed for. In response they sometimes see a spontaneous spiritually transforming work of the Holy Spirit in their midst. They become like parents, excited about seeing someone's new life in Christ take root, develop, and mature.

The Holy Spirit is doing something profound, powerful, and important.

In many cases these new believers come to the corporate worship services. There they often make a public profession of the faith they had more privately embraced in the context of a small, caring group where their needs were met.

In the next 12 months, one out of every four church-related small groups across North America will win someone to faith in Christ.

Such testimonies represent the heartbeat of our Christian calling: People showing love to people who are seeking Christ, who are coming to Him, and who are becoming a part of God's family, all under the blessing of and in "shared ministry" with the pastoral staff. As God saves people, he wants to use both clergy and "non-clergy" of the congregation as His instruments!

Could That Be *Your* Group?

In the next 12 months, one out of every four church-related small groups across North America will win someone to faith in Christ. Your group can be part of that disciple-making harvest even if you're not an evangelist. In fact, it doesn't matter whether your group meets in homes or at your church's facilities. You may call yourselves a Sunday school class, a Bible study, a care group, a task team, or something else. What's important is not your group's name, but that you develop caring, nurturing relationships marked by one-another ministry (to be explained further in Key Five). In an environment like that, people are virtually "loved" into the Kingdom of God.

What's important is not your group's name, but that you develop caring, nurturing relationships marked by one-another ministry.

But an even more important dynamic is at issue: groups like this can't exist until a leader has been raised up, trained, and empowered. Stated positively, *the more ministry-capable leaders there are, the more quality groups a church can sponsor*. Each additional ministry

6

group represents a place where more and better disciples can mature. In short, the most effective strategy for fulfilling many commands of Scripture is for a church to place priority on *making disciplemakers*.

The most effective strategy for fulfilling many commands of Scripture is for a church to place priority on *making disciplemakers*.

In churches of the future, whether small or big, the pastoral team will increasingly give attention to training and releasing volunteer ministers—people like you! Churches will be known for doing "small" well. This idea is nothing new; groups and teams of 5-15 people, effectively networked together, are fundamental to virtually every healthy church around the world.

Groups and teams of 5-15 people, effectively networked together, are fundamental to virtually every healthy church around the world.

In churches of the future, ministry leaders will place priority on reproducing themselves. The principle of 2 Timothy 2:2—in essence, raising up leaders who can reproduce themselves in others—will become more central to the mission and strategy of any church that wishes to increase its impact in outreach, care, and discipleship.

Nine Keys to Effective Small Group Leadership will help you see how *your leadership role* can make a huge difference for the cause of Christ. You'll be part of a revolution that revolves around one core truth: If your group or team is marked by a contagious love, then people will want to join it. As a result, more and better disciples will be made. In short, the key to evangelism with durable fruit is a lay-shepherded small community that convincingly demonstrates Christ's compelling love. And the secret of having enough such communities of faith is a leader who learns to make not only disciples but also other disciplemakers.

If your group or team is marked by a contagious love, then ...more and better disciples will be made.

Is God calling your group to model a persuasive, Christ-like love? Is God calling you to multiply the kind of leaders who convene new groups? If so, expect a waiting line for your group—and a church transformed from the bottom up. Whatever kind of group you lead, these transferable principles will help it become more effective in evangelism and renewal, as well as in making more and better disciplemakers.

CHAPTER

2

YOU SERVE A POWERFUL GOD

WHAT'S THE BIBLICAL BASIS BEHIND THE POWER OF GROUPS? It's very basic. Jesus said that wherever two or three gather in His name, He is there in the midst (see Matthew 18:20, NKJV). This promise speaks of a meeting ("gathered together") with an agenda ("in my name") that is blessed with Christ's presence ("in the midst"). This time-space event with namable individuals and a properly constructed plan draws a presence of God that is not promised elsewhere in the Bible.

When Christians come together in the name of the Lord Jesus, there is a special sense of His presence—a sacrament of sorts in the sense of outward and visible signs of inward and spiritual graces. As believers provoke one another to love and good works, a wonderful atmosphere of camaraderie, fellowship, belonging, and caring comes to the group. Beautiful expressions of the Holy Spirit also take place as a person with one set of spiritual gifts interacts with those who have received other gifts.

Church growth occurs when new converts or new seekers come into

9

that setting. They listen to the integrity, honesty, and love of these Christians as they try to work out their faith.

The consequences are wonderful indeed. When seekers enter a small group and watch the love that Christians demonstrate to each other, something happens that reduces their resistance to the gospel, causes them to open their hearts to the love of God, and enables them to receive Christ. The net result is that Jesus gets through to these people!

...something happens that reduces their resistance to the gospel.

Elsewhere Jesus told his followers: Here's how people will know that you are my disciples "if you have love one for another" (John 13:35). Not "if you have truth adequately worded in doctrine," as important as that may be. Rather, Christians are told to offer more than the words of the gospel to an unbelieving world; we must also offer participation in a small Christian community that is a manifestation of Christ's ongoing work through the Body of Christ.

Christians are told to offer more than the words of the gospel to an unbelieving world; we must also offer participation in a small Christian community ...a manifestation of the Body of Christ.

That's why we are best able to demonstrate the love of Christ one to another through a framework of caring units. As we learn how to go about "speaking the truth in love" (Ephesians 4:15) in a context of Biblical community, truth wields a powerful effect as people's lives are changed.

The bottom line: your small group is an essential tool for ministry to people.

What You Mean by "Small Group"
Virtually every church across our globe does the majority of its ministry through groups. In simplest form *a small group is a face-to-*

face meeting that is a sub-unit of the overall fellowship. To have a distinctive identity, these meetings probably need to convene two or more times in a typical month.

A small group is a face-to-face meeting that is a sub-unit of the overall fellowship.

Regardless of what the group is named, certain generic qualities tend to show up when God's people are meeting together in Jesus' name for ministry. As a result, the principles of this book can apply to all of the following group types (and no doubt others we've forgotten to include). *Pastoral care can occur under any of these names:*

- Adult Children of Alcoholics Support Group
- Agape Cell
- Aging Parents Support Group
- Basic Christian Community
- Bible Study
- Body Life Group
- Care Circle
- Care Units
- Care Clusters
- Care Group
- Care Team
- Cell Group
- Class Meeting
- Community Fellowship Group
- Cottage Prayer Group
- Covenant Group
- Covenant Network
- Deacon Board
- Door Group
- Elder Board
- Fellowship Flock
- F.I.R.E. Group (Friends In Relational Evangelism)
- F.I.S.H. Group (Fellowship In Someone's Home)
- Flock Group

- Friendship Group
- Governance Group
- Grace Group
- Growth Group
- H.E.A.R.T. Group (Home, Encouragement, Accountability, Relationships, and Teaching)
- Home Cell Ministry
- Home Fellowship Group
- H.O.M.E. Group (Homes, Open for Ministry and Encouragement or Helping Others Mature Eternally)
- I.C.U.s (Intensive Care Units)
- Intercession Center
- Intergenerational Group
- L.I.F.E. Group (Loving Individuals through Fellowship and Evangelism or Living In Faith Everyday or Living In Fullness Everyday)
- Martha's Helpers Missions Group
- Neighborhood Bible Fellowships
- Newlyweds Support Group
- Nurture Group
- Power House
- Prison Ministry Task Group
- Pulpit Group
- Recovery Group
- Shepherd Group
- Small Sunday School Class
- Support Group
- T.L.C. Group (Tender Loving Care)
- Twelve-Step Group
- Yokefellow Circle

Reality 101 in Your Church

If the church you attend is typical, there are lots of job or ministry "hats" constantly available to you through the various sub-units of the overall church:

• "Our soup kitchen team needs someone to coordinate the Meals on Wheels volunteers."

- "As the new Promise Keepers coordinator, Tom Johnston is looking for a leader to assist him. Anyone interested?"
- "Wouldn't it be great if someone started an outreach to that new housing development near our church building?"
- "We would have a number from the Junior High Choir at this point in our service if we had a director for that group."
- "Which Sunday school class wants to sponsor the Memorial Day picnic this year?"
- "Pleeeease! Your church needs more volunteers in the nursery!"

The principles of this book can help you be more effective no matter which of these groups you serve as a ministry leader. If you have accepted a leadership hat, or plan to do so in the near future, then this book can help you be more effective in that role.

More important, *Nine Keys to Effective Small Group Leadership* can train you in new perspectives and skills of discipling others, especially other future leaders. Jesus' final command on earth, known as the Great Commission, was to "make disciples" (Matthew 28:19-20). The following chapters talk about nine crucial dimensions of that process— nine frameworks for your personal ministry, nine ways to reproduce in others what God has done in you, nine keys to growing effective ministry groups.

These Biblically informed marching orders will help you create caring communities of faith and leadership development. When energized by the Holy Spirit, they will serve as a charter showing you how to make an incredible difference for Christ.

3

CHAPTER

WHO ARE YOU LEADING?

I BEGAN TO LEARN THE SIGNIFICANCE OF LEADERSHIP JUST AFTER graduate school, when I was a youth pastor in Florida. I was riding with a busload of teens headed to a week-long summer camp. In the hours before we left, one after another of our adult sponsors faced emergencies that required them to cancel. The handful of us who remained could barely cover legal, safety, and chaperoning needs. However, this sudden reduction in the number of adult counselors meant our high schoolers would have to be largely self-supervised in their cabins and between scheduled activities.

Lesson from a Young Frontierswoman

The situation made a great climate for urgent intercession! Sitting there on the back seat of the bus, I had to figure out a quick makeshift plan. I needed to group the kids together in such a way that when we had chapel or roll call, I could have confidence they'd show up.

After some foxhole praying, I hit upon a plan. I'd select the kids I knew to be leaders. I'd put their names on a list, one per cabin, and let all the other teens sign up under them.

I began scanning the bus rows in front of me. "There's a leader," I

15

told myself. "Those two are leaders," I said as I wrote down various names.

I paused at one of the girls. "She's a leader," I thought to myself, "but she's not exemplary as a spiritually minded person." So I left her off the leader list.

When we arrived at camp, all the young people assigned themselves to cabins based on the leaders I had selected en route. The teen-assisted leadership system worked well for several days. Then came a chapel service with a big gap in the bleachers. Almost 20 girls out of the 100 total high schoolers were missing.

After finding their cabin empty, we sent out a search party. Soon enough we spotted 15 to 18 girls coming out of the woods, still in their nighties and hair up in curlers. They were completely out of our control but obviously having a wonderful time wandering about.

After making sure everyone was accounted for and safe, I sized up who the ringleader was. It was the girl whose name I had omitted from the leadership list.

I pulled her aside and said, "That was quite an amazing adventure this morning. I haven't seen leadership like that in a long time. Can we talk?"

"What about?" she answered.

"I think I need your help in running this camp," I admitted.

"It's about time you woke up to that," she replied with a grin.

"Would you accept the responsibility of being a group leader?" I asked. "Could you get your cabin mates to chapel without detouring through the woods? I think you have that kind of ability."

Whether or not I named her as a leader, she influenced the behavior of others.

She agreed to my charge. The kids under her influence quickly fell into line. I think she grew spiritually in the process. She accepted my supervision and rose to the occasion.

She was clearly a natural leader, although not in spiritual matters at that time. Whether or not I named her as a leader, she influenced the behavior of others. Wherever she went, someone followed her.

Are You Leading–Or Just Taking a Walk?

I've reflected on that event numerous times over the years. It illustrates a number of principles visible in most churches.

This young "frontierswoman" reminds me that if you don't have a literal, physical following, you don't have leadership. Leaders, by definition, have followers. If you call a meeting and no one comes, you may go by the title of leader, whether "Sunday school teacher" or "Promise Keepers group facilitator" or whatever, but you aren't leading.

...if you don't have a literal, physical following, you don't have leadership.

At our church high school camp, I had designated several youths as cabin leaders because of their personal maturity in Christ. Some of them, who were also graced with God-given leadership traits, did fine. Others were follower types. Some of these joined the natural leader in trekking through the woods. It was a mistake for me to think that spirituality overcomes leadership deficits—or that spirituality equals leadership.

On the other hand, if I as a youth pastor could get actual leaders involved, and also receive their permission to work on their spiritual lives, then they would help me bring along the rest of the group. In three decades of observations since that event, I've concluded that every church contains many leaders with unrecognized potential, such as this teenage girl represented.

My prayer as you read the following chapters is that you will join in the important task of seeking out leaders with unrecognized potential. I invite you to play a role in growing with them as they become effective agents for broadening the ministry impact of your church.

INTRODUCTION TO PART 2

THE FOLLOWING PAGES CONTAIN NINE KEYS TO INCREASE YOUR effectiveness as a group leader. May they be tools that simplify your life and provide greater focus to your ministry. May they offer helpful steps you can begin to take this week. May they also suggest a cohesive game plan that will lead you into a whole new way of understanding how God works through your church and others.

What does a healthy partnership between a pastor and a lay worker look like? The lay minister will be encouraged, helped, and empowered to do the following:

1. Check in with the church staff so they will view you as a partner in ministry.
2. Recruit your replacement, even before you hold your first meeting.
3. Keep reaching out between meetings, cultivating new contacts.
4. Prepare for every meeting in prayer and by involving your apprentice.
5. Conduct your meeting, keeping it on track.
6. Bring your people to worship for your weekend services.
7. Teach people how to give to and serve each other as well as those outside the group.
8. Do evangelism from the group by building bridges of friendship with the unchurched.
9. Stay before the Lord, deepening your own spiritual life of faith.

The section you're about to read—the main body of *Nine Keys to Effective Small Group Leadership*—shows what you can do to develop each of these vital skills.

19

CONNECT

 Connect: Build a strong link with the pastoral staff.

Recruit:

Invite:

Prepare:

Meet:

Bring:

Serve:

Win:

Seek:

CHAPTER

4

KEY ONE:
CONNECT WITH THE LEADERSHIP
NETWORK IN YOUR CHURCH

CHAPTER SUMMARY

How to Connect:
☑ 1. Accept leadership responsibility for your group.
☑ 2. Establish goals for your group.
☑ 3. Be available for individual and/or group coaching
　　　sessions.
☑ 4. Cooperate with the coaching process.
☑ 5. Understand how respect for authority strengthens
　　　faith.

S UPPOSE SOMEONE ASKS YOU TO DESCRIBE THE CHURCH YOU
attend. Chances are, as you begin talking about the people who
make up the church, you'll sooner or later reference two
longstanding, widely used categories. One grouping has names like
clergy, pastor, pulpit minister, priest, father, bishop, church staff

21

member, or cleric. Churches usually pay these full- or part-time people as trained professionals. The other group, generally made up of volunteers, in fact do a great deal of the work of the church, if not most of the work. The most common term used to describe them begins with the word *lay*, as in laity, layman, laywoman, or layperson.

Volunteers ...do a great deal of the work of the church, if not most of the work.

As you may know, the word *laity* (meaning "non-clergy people") is a distinction unknown to the early church. Instead, the New Testament's names for followers of Christ are "disciples," "saints," "servants," "believers," and "chosen ones," among others. Such people have an awesome calling: to use the gifts and fruit of the Spirit to do the work of ministry as Christ's representatives here on earth (see Ephesians 4:12-16 and Galatians 5:22-23).

Those are noble titles and responsibilities indeed! By contrast, you sometimes hear someone say, somewhat apologetically, "My role at church? I'm just a layman." The negative implication is "I'm not important" or "I'm second-class." Hopefully, after reading this book, you'll never again be tempted to mumble, "I'm just a volunteer minister."

Further, these confusing terms point to another myth: that churches won't get better until there are more clergy to go around. The real problem in most churches stems from the belief that the ministry of care is the job of the clergy and not all God's people. Current levels of need are caused by the failure of the family as a support system to provide that care (see chapter 13). The nurture that came from extended family, the interactions that accompanied a life spent in one small community, and the training in parenting and homemaking skills, simply aren't valued or practiced today at the same level as in yesteryear.

Most churches have not compensated for these societal changes. The typical congregation has not yet developed a comprehensive system of pastoral care.

One possible solution involves rebuilding the foundations of society through the group life of each local church. The generic term for those tiny, foundational units is *cell group*—an analogy taken from cells as the basic units of life. Cells go by such names as home Bible study, small Sunday school class (if it takes time to listen as well as to teach), work team, or board (if it takes time to pray for one another as well as to focus on its task). John Wesley called them "class meetings" and "little companies," John Wimber calls them "spiritual kinship groups," and David Yonggi Cho (formerly Paul Yonggi Cho) calls them a "home cell group system." Whatever their name, each one (if they're healthy) plays an important part in fleshing out such key theological values as "community" and "one-another ministry."

Jesus told His small group, "By this all men will know that you are my disciples, if you love one another" (John 13:35). Those words seem to imply that interactions in community accredits a group as His disciples, and therefore suitable for His work.

Why does that idea make sense? If the "work" of your group depends on the spiritual strength and emotional health of each person who co-labors with you, then the most fundamental contribution your leadership can make is to make sure all persons in your charge are being helped to good health by being "pastored" by fellow members in the group.

Scripture characterizes small-group ministry by one-another mutuality. In the New Testament, ministry is described as something believers do "together." In at least 59 different places in the New Testament (see Key Five, pages 106-107) believers are commanded to love one another, encourage one another, forgive one another, bear one another's burdens, and in many other ways provide mutual "one another" pastoral care. Each person you build up has the potential to instill something in your own life that's every bit as precious and valuable to you as your encouragement is to them.

Leaders Accept Certain Responsibilities

The leader represents a key starting point for pulling together a group. Building on that perspective, here is a very basic model of ministry: the

How to Connect #1: Accept leadership responsibility for your group.

"fullness of Christ" (Ephesians 4:13) occurs in a special way when a spiritually minded leader pulls together a small gathering of people in Jesus' name. The Lord Jesus manifests Himself in their midst (Matthew 18:20) and they see Jesus in one another. As they love each other, new people are drawn toward Christ. Everyone present participates in a disciple-shaping process, especially those involved in new-leader formation. As priority is placed on the disciplemaking of leaders in training, they, in turn, make possible the creating of new witnessing communities of faith. That's what this book is all about—*Nine Keys to Effective Small Group Leadership: how lay leaders can establish dynamic and healthy cells, classes, or teams.*

The "fullness of Christ" occurs in a special way ...in small groups.

When a disciplemaking rhythm is put into motion, it takes a church beyond anything imagined, returning it to the very foundations of church health seen in the book of Acts. The cycle starts when someone accepts responsibility for being a blessing to people who are seeking God, who are seeking help, who are seeking comfort, and who are seeking to make something worthwhile of their lives.

The principles that follow apply whether you are part of a service team, ministry task force, a home group, Bible study, a regular gathering that has breakfast together, or a small Sunday school class. Any gathering of less than a dozen people is a small group. If that group meets because someone is calling it together, it is an intentionally led group.

Leaders Have Goals for Their Group

How to Connect #2:

Establish goals for your group.

All groups have distinct aims in accordance with their purpose. A musical ensemble may seek to master a new song by next weekend's worship service. A Mothers-of-Preschoolers prayer meeting fulfills its mission by sponsoring a time of intercession for its youngsters. A twelve-step group will deal with one or more recovery steps at virtually every

24

meeting. A Bible study spends part of its regular meeting time learning and applying the Scriptures.

Some groups will use a contract or covenant to clarify expectations and commitments of members one to another. Agreed-on common behaviors might include a confidentiality policy: "Whatever is said here, stays here." Other elements might include pledges of regular group attendance and participation, weekly homework, accountability, openness to newcomers, or daily prayer for each other.

These devices are sometimes written and signed by all members; other times they are created and reaffirmed verbally. In leadership development contexts, additional, more specific contracts or covenants occur between the leader and apprentices to outline their special relationship of training and mentoring.

Each Group Is Part of Something Bigger

Your job as leader, under God and as a servant of Jesus Christ, begins by taking responsibility for bringing people together (Key Two) and for seeing to it that you're on the right track as you provide leadership to them (Keys Three through Nine). That initiating role is necessary, whatever the specific charter of your group.

However, your role as leader also addresses an objective even bigger than your group's specific purpose. Through your group, you are exercising a stewardship of the pastoral office. If we, as lay ministers, do not extend the Great Shepherd's care within our groups, then the fullness of love Christ wants to show His church will not be fully manifest.

Lay ministers ...extend the Great Shepherd's care within our groups.

Therefore, as you take responsibility for your group, you are doing more than facilitating a Bible study, convening a prayer group, leading a team that clothes the homeless, teaching a Sunday-school lesson, and the like. You are serving as a helper to other people's spiritual development, even as they strengthen you on your own faith journey.

ꙨꙨ

You need to have this dream that says, "I want to be a blessing to someone."

ꙨꙨ

You need to have this dream that says, "I want to be a blessing to someone." If that is your motivation, then it's very appropriate, whatever group you lead, to set a faith-development goal: "I will, under the guidance of the Holy Spirit and under the coaching of the church staff, become a ministry leader who convenes about ten people at a time and pours myself into those people's lives so that they become fully recognizable as committed Christians. They will be recognized as God's people."

ꙨꙨ

Your job as a leader includes helping them become all Jesus Christ wants them to be.

ꙨꙨ

Your job as leader includes helping them become all Jesus Christ wants them to be—and can help them become.

All Leaders Need a Ministry Supervisor

To reach maximum effectiveness in these goals, you cannot function independently from the rest of the church body. The rest of this chapter will highlight three reasons why.

In hundreds of consultations across dozens of denominations, I have heard cries for a shared ministry. The ideal is this: Professional clergy, who are well-trained theologically and administratively, make their resources available to volunteer leaders who want to be of help to others.

How to Connect #3: Be available for individual and/or group coaching sessions.

In most cases, the easiest way to develop or strengthen such a shared partnership is for you, as a volunteer worker, to connect with the formal ministry power structure of your congregation. If you don't link properly with the official authority in your church, you may be looked upon as a renegade or outlaw, somebody who gives the pastoral staff a certain discomfort, leaving them uncertain about what's happening "out there." Any pastor who hasn't personally watched a small group divisively jump ship and affiliate en masse with a church—or cult—down the street, has undoubtedly heard such horror stories from fellow clergy. Scripture charges your pastor with oversight of your soul (1 Peter 2:25). It also cautions you and me not to give grief to our shepherds (2 Corinthians 2:2-5), but rather to be good followers of those who have been assigned authority over us (Hebrews 13:17).

You also want to avoid any smack of an attitude that invites fear among your church's governance structure or otherwise says to it, "We don't need you." After all, the purpose of ministry is to edify the Body of Christ, strengthening one part in order to contribute health to the whole (see Ephesians 4). As God's church works as one, then the world will take note and believe (see John 17).

Without a good connection to someone in authority ...you might be viewed with more suspicion than appreciation.

Your group life may be the most real thing that happens outside the Communion or preaching event. However, without a good connection to someone in authority, either on church staff or someone designated by those in authority, you might be viewed with more suspicion than appreciation. That trust factor is the first reason why you need to be connected to the leadership network of your church.

Leaders Don't Like to Feel Abandoned

Perhaps more important from your perspective is this second reason: a lack of connection may cause you to feel overlooked, left out, abandoned or unimportant. Consider, for example, the following supposed conversation:

"How's your group going?" Bill asked Tony as they walked from the church parking lot toward their Sunday-morning worship service.

"Great!" Tony replied. "I think this will be our best year yet."

"How's that?" Bill probed, thinking about the lack of momentum in his own group.

"A year ago, I felt all alone. Sure, Doris would listen to me at home after the meetings. But I didn't think our Care Group mattered to anyone at church."

"You mean to Pastor Bob and the church board?" asked Bill as they continued walking slowly toward the church building.

"It was like we were a floating ministry," explained Tony. "God has carried every couple in our group through a major job change during the two years we've met. That's great stuff, but because we don't meet in the church building, we didn't seem to feel included or fit in. We didn't feel we were a fully legitimate ministry."

"Then how did the pastor find out about the answered prayer he described in last week's sermon? It was about a recently divorced woman who felt so welcome in your group."

"That's because we got connected, and it made a big difference."

"Sounds like signing onto a long-distance company," chuckled Bill.

"Not at all," Tony continued. "A few months back I was chatting with the pastor after church one Sunday. He asked me who I go to for advice and encouragement about my group. His schedule is so full that I didn't want to add another burden. So I told him our group didn't have any great need."

By now the men had stopped walking and were standing together beside the sanctuary doors.

"What changed?" asked Bill.

"Pastor asked if I'd try something," answered Tony. "You know Albert Wong, don't you? Al's led groups for years, and he and I get along well. Pastor asked if Al could serve as a coach to me. Al would come to the meeting once in a while, he'd pray for me during the week, and he'd keep the pastor regularly updated on our group.

"Al has phoned or met with me almost every week since then. Actually, Al is doing that for three or four different groups. Once in a while he gets the leaders from all four groups together to talk about what we're learning."

"You don't feel like Al is checking up on you?" asked Bill.

"It's really helpful to have that level of accountability," said Tony. "I know Al talks regularly with Pastor Bob, because that's how the pastor heard about our latest answered prayer. Our whole group feels like we're part of the big picture now."

"Good to hear," said Bill. "Maybe Al needs to adopt me too! My prayer group at work doesn't seem to be going anywhere."

"Pastor says it works best when our coach is someone we already know and look up to," said Tony. "Why not ask Pastor who the other coaches are? Maybe there's somebody you know better than Al."

"Thanks," said Bill. "We'd better go inside or our wives will tease us about getting lost in the parking lot."

You Have at Least 800,000 Peers

Stories like that are repeating themselves in thousands of churches. Across North America more people are part of off-premises groups than ever before. According to a Lily Endowment-Gallup Poll, some 15-20 million people, for example, meet during any given month in some 800,000 Bible study groups that include mutual pastoral care. In fact, there are now more off-campus, church-related groups in North America than on-premises Sunday school classes. Today's small-group movement is so broad, covering everything from Sunday school classes to prayer groups, from nurture groups to Bible study groups, that it almost defies definition.

Some 15-20 million people ...meet during any given month in some 800,000 Bible study groups that include mutual pastoral care.

Even among all this diversity, an increasing number of group leaders are finding benefit in having a legitimate connection point with the church staff. A growing number are building a healthy relationship with the staff member or supervisor who takes their report and coaches them. They appreciate having someone designated to be there when they want to report on what's happening in their group as well as for resourcing and support.

Leaders Welcome a Coach's Input

What shape would a verbal reporting session take? Let's imagine the following telephone conversation between Jan (a coach) and Heidi (a group leader):

JAN: Heidi, so glad we could talk. How are you?

HEIDI: Glad to sit down for a few minutes. It's been a busy day. We had a power outage at work, which threw everything into a tizzy.

JAN: And the family? What's new on the home front?

HEIDI: Thanks for asking. The boys are coming home for the weekend, so it should be a good time. We're all looking forward to it.

JAN: How did your group go this week?

HEIDI: Attendance was way down, but God gave a very special time to those who came.

How to
Connect
#4:
Cooperate with the
coaching process.

JAN: Tell me more. What made it so special?

HEIDI: We get closer every week. We've really become friends. We feel like we can be transparent with each other.

JAN: That's terrific. Sounds like your group meets a lot of needs.

HEIDI: It does. I just wish more people would come.

JAN: Am I hearing that one of your dreams is to build the attendance?

HEIDI: Sure, but I don't know what we can do.

JAN: In your group, Sarah is your leader in training, right?

HEIDI: Yes, though she's been ill the last two meetings.

JAN: Have you and Sarah talked and prayed about how to build the attendance?

HEIDI: Talked, yes; prayed, probably not enough. She and I have each sort of targeted one other person to invite.

JAN: So you've got two prospects that you're working on.

HEIDI: We also use an open chair at our meetings as a symbol to remind our whole group that we'd like it to be filled with newcomers.

JAN: How are you keeping connections going with these two people?

HEIDI: It's hard to keep relating to them, but we both sense it's the right thing to do.

JAN: If it's the right thing to do, what if you did more of it? Suppose you each did something with *three* new people and then invited each one to next week's meeting?

HEIDI: I suppose we'd be three times as likely to be turned down!

JAN: I heard some feeling behind that comment.

HEIDI: Just kidding. You're asking if maybe we need to fish in a bigger stream.

JAN: Well, you keep telling me that God is doing some neat things in the group, which you wish others could be part of.

HEIDI: I do. Do other group leaders have this same frustration with bringing in newcomers?

JAN: Sometimes. At one of our coaches' training sessions we watched and discussed a video that gave us a 1-to-2 principle: if you want to have 8 people at the meeting, you'll need to be cultivating 15 to 20 at one level or another.

HEIDI: Wow. Maybe Sarah and I have been unrealistic in our expectations.

JAN: Whether you have or haven't, you're doing a great job. Why don't you and Sarah, when you talk before next meeting, see whether God wants to bring several more names to your minds? Then prayerfully look for an opportunity to serve or meet with them.

HEIDI: It's worth a try.

JAN: Anything else you'd like me to pray for as I think about you?

HEIDI: Sarah's health. She really wants to feel better so she will be able to attend the meetings. And how can I pray for you?

JAN: Be glad to tell you. Then, do you have a few minutes where we could pray together...?

That conversation could have spanned five minutes or an hour. The important factor is that these two people:

- got reconnected,
- celebrated successes,
- debriefed a bit, affirming key values represented in those successes,
- set new goals, figured out what obstacles needed to be overcome, and
- left with specific action steps to take before the next meeting.

Coaches want their group leaders to receive a vision of the future that's even better than where they've just been.

31

Coaches want their group leaders to receive a vision of the future that's even better than where they've just been. Coaches rejoice with whatever helps a group gain another inch forward.

Heidi left that meeting recharged and looking forward to the upcoming week. Jan gave her reinforcing feedback on what worked well and also a small dose of formative feedback to use in planning for her next week's meeting.

If you want to benefit from the coaching process, learn to be easy on yourself in the opening phases of a consultation, and during your closing minutes be intentional about what you'll do next time. Don't focus on what didn't go so well, beating yourself up with your coach. Nothing's harder than to work with a person who feels defeated, or is naturally self-flagellating with all the negatives about their ministry. You can't get their psychological powerbase built up to the point that they can accept an honest affirmation. "No, I messed up so badly, you don't understand..." people like this will moan.

Rather, be willing to celebrate successes. Nurture yourself to the point of strength. Early in the coaching process, don't take on too many issues.

I've watched athletic coaches work with our sons in track and field events. Champion coaches don't raise the high-jump bar two feet at a time; they add one inch or maybe two. They keep bragging on the athletes each time they meet a new challenge. In other track and field events, I've seen my sons' discus throw go a few feet farther than their previous personal best. With more coaching, they then beat that new record as well.

Champion [athletic] coaches don't raise the high-jump bar two feet at a time; they add one inch or maybe two.

In the mind of the athlete, there's a direct relationship between praise and goal setting. Most kids don't believe they can throw the javelin as far as their coach wants them to.

The coach will say, "I was watching you carefully, and if you'd put a little more energy in the first two seconds of your throw, I believe you could add three or four feet."

"You really think so, Coach?" the youth will reply.

"Dad, my coach thinks I could throw it five feet farther," the youth may report after the next practice. The accomplishment grows with the dream, the imagination, the practice, and the feedback.

If you're meeting fairly regularly with a coach or ministry supervisor, then you should notice gradual gains in your effectiveness. Even small gains, when added regularly and incrementally like compound interest, lead to superb leadership skills over time.

Small gains, when added regularly and incrementally, lead to superb leadership skills over time.

Some churches not only encourage verbal report-taking like what happened between Heidi and Jan, but they also use forms to guide the coaches as they take reports.

What does a written report look like? Generally it generates a structured discussion based on certain leading indicators. Often it's the coach who does the writing, based on such interview questions as:

• What are some good things that are happening to the people in your care?

• What progress are you seeing in your apprentice; in identifying additional rising apprentices?

• How many seekers or newcomers were present at your last meetings?

• How many meetings ago did a coach or staff member visit your group or team meeting?

• What's next for your group?

• What's next in your own leadership development?*

If you want to be most effective in growing and changing your ministry, you need to learn how to cooperate with the coaching process. The tone of the relationship is very important for people's well-being. Coaching needs to be an uplifting and positive experience.

You don't want hit-or-miss caring in the church any more than when you go to the hospital do you want hit-or-miss medical attention!

---

* Contact Carl George (P.O. Box 5407, Diamond Bar, California, 91765-5407, phone 909-396-6843, or fax 909-396-6845) for a free copy of a widely used structured interview for debriefing.

Whether you're at church or the doctor's, you probably want an extensively trained staff. Why? Their process of care will give a consistently better result than would haphazard care.

For thousands of years ...the deacons took care of the crises, and "Mom" took care of everything else.

Unfortunately, many churches have not spent much energy on assured care issues. For generations, "Mom" took care of those matters through the home. For centuries the theological community has depended on "Mom" to do much of the pastoral caring. The deacons took care of the crises, and "Mom" took care of everything else. In the post World War II generation, women went to work, families became smaller, and mobility tore families apart. "Mom" is no longer filling that nurturing, community-building role at the same level she once was.

In response to these societal changes, a church must be very deliberate about encouraging care. It can no longer assume it will happen automatically.

Coaches Are Often Veteran Group Leaders

What kind of person might end up as your ministry supervisor, if you plug yourself into your church staff? In smaller churches you might directly report to the senior pastor. In larger churches, your point of contact may be a pastoral-care staff person.

Both of those arrangements will last only the first year or two in an expanding small-group ministry. More likely over time, your actual reporting will occur with a volunteer who is somewhat like an athletic coach, whose team is a handful of small-group leaders. This person typically works with leaders of no more than five small groups. Coaches who try to handle more than this amount usually run out of space in their lives. They become overworked and can't do the job needed.

The person serving as a coach often gathers a handful of cell leaders to do the report-taking as a group. This approach is similar to a football huddle where the players meet together with their quarter back.

Although many churches find it helpful to use this leadership huddle model, the analogy breaks down at one point: Usually not every group leader can make it to a huddle meeting. If life contained no sick children, no late nights at work, no vacation travel, and no other similarly complicating circumstances, then it would be possible to think that the coach's job is limited to conducting huddle meetings. A good percentage of cell leaders might get to a huddle session, but those who don't still need coaching. If you're going to have an effective ministry, there must be a frequent, purposeful contact between the coach and the person giving the report. It can occur in a group or one-on-one, but churches that are effective in increasing the number of people under care in small groups have learned they can't leave coaching to chance.

Churches that are effective in increasing the number of people under care in small groups have learned they can't leave coaching to chance.

Coaches, much like cell leaders, take responsibility for the care of leaders even more than for the convening of leadership meetings. In general, coaches seek to touch base with the group leaders under their care at least once every week. If a group leader doesn't show up for a huddle meeting, then the coach makes a lunch appointment or picks up the phone and makes contact one-on-one. It's not the group leaders' attendance at a huddle meeting that counts, so much as the quality of nurture and support they receive.

At our home, a little poodle meets me at the door. He's never paid a bill; in fact he represents an investment in my veterinarian's ability to underwrite his children's college tuition fees! Our puppy has been run over by a truck and munched on by a big dog down the street. Between his stays at the animal hospital, he damaged things with his teething and broke several household items.

Why, then, do we like him so much? He's excited about greeting people! When any of us comes in the door, he treats the family like we're the most special people in the world. Perhaps we can learn a lot from the puppy in how we treat each other.

A healthy coaching relationship can build the same positive expectation as I have when I see our puppy: I look forward to the experience because he always affirms me so effectively. Likewise, part of a coach's responsibility is to make the leaders feel like the most special people in the world.

Sometimes It's Not Easy to Find the Right Person

Perhaps you belong to a church where the Lone Ranger, with his aversion to being known, would feel comfortable. Maybe the pastoral team takes little initiative to connect with its volunteer force. Possibly most of the lay leaders don't have much interest in anything that looks like supervision.

It is still *your* responsibility to make a report so they know what's going on with you! You need to find those in spiritual authority and say, "Okay, who do I give a ministry report to?"

The reason you have to ask around in some churches is because there's not always been much forethought given to being a ministry supervisor. The typical pastor has received little if any training in formal management; usually those on church staff with good management skills either have a God-given talent in that area or else they learned it outside traditional paths for clergy education. In other words, you should expect to offer to help! This is another reason why the structured interview for debriefing (see footnote on page 33) might be helpful in your church.

Your pastor or church leadership team may well be deeply interested in you, but simply not know how to express it. Assume the best motives on their part. Meanwhile, keep taking the initiative to stay connected.

Leadership Cautions for Support and Recovery Groups

All the teachings of this book apply to addiction recovery groups, such as "divorce recovery" or "grief recovery." However the leaders of such groups have additional factors to consider because they're in a quasi-mental health area.

Support group leaders likewise face many problems that border on the kinds of dysfunctions and issues attended to in mental health therapy environments. In support groups, the volunteer lay leader is a friend, a collaborator, and a person coming alongside participants. The group leader is not presuming to be competent in mental health areas. Problems may surface that are out of the leader's skill range. These matters will need to be referred to professionals for more formalized evaluation and therapy. Coaches and group leaders alike need help on learning how to answer, "Is this problem out of range for me?" and "Does this person's need require a competency out of my range?"

Knowing where that line is to be drawn will require counsel from a coach conversant on these issues. Coaches for small group leaders must either be mental health professionals or have access to them. One of the challenges a church staff faces is to provide that quality of resource to support and recovery group coaches. It's usually arranged through a contract with a mental health practitioner who will schedule regular debriefing sessions with counselors and support group leaders.

Because of the litigious nature of our society, organizations like Rapha have prepared resources to help churches avoid problems in this area. One such kit they designed to help churches safeguard their support and recovery ministries is the *Liability Management Notebook for Pastoral Counselors*, by George Ohlschlager, Peter Mosgofian, Kevin C. Rodgers, and Stuart Rothberg. The material addresses everything from confidentiality to referral to leadership training. (For more information contact Baxter Press, phone 281-992-0628, fax 281-992-0615, mail 700 S. Friendswood Dr. Suite B, Friendswood, TX 77546).

Leaders Need to Be Empowered and Legitimized

There is a third and perhaps most important reason why it is vital that you, as a group leader, find someone to whom you can report regularly. If you want to be empowered for ministry, then you need to work under legitimate authority. That ongoing sense of a license is even more important than holding the meeting. Why? If you are operating under legitimate authority, then you have a right to

How to Connect #5: Understand how respect for authority strengthens faith.

ask others to follow you. You're also not likely to misdirect them. Even if you started to mislead them, the fact that you're making reports gives those in leadership over you an opportunity to shape your direction and introduce correctives.

> ## If you are operating under legitimate authority, then you have a right to ask others to follow you.

Leaders Grow in Faith, Maturity, and Skill

Sometimes a church hits a wall when trying to create an empowered climate for ministry development. The pastoral leadership, having preached on "priesthood of all believers" texts from Scripture, is surprised that many professionally educated people refuse to take roles in the context of the church's volunteer ministry. The reason? Not that they're unwilling to be obedient to God. Rather, they take spiritual matters *so* seriously that they're afraid to step forward.

Listen to this dentist who spoke with me: "I spent years learning how to drill teeth before I did permanent work on anyone's mouth. An unskilled first-year dental student can do a lot of irrevocable damage with a drill, you know! As important as teeth are, they're nothing compared to marriages, career decisions, and other issues that come up in a cell group. Without adequate training and backup, how am I to care for human souls?"

Regular, quality supervision can build on basic training and compensate for a lack of extensive training. If supervision is constant or frequent, then those taking the cell leader's report can guard against divisiveness, cultish tendencies, or spiritual lethargy. Together they can trust God to speak through the group on relationship matters and life stage issues. Week by week they can celebrate God's goodness as people are gently and lovingly brought to truth through a legitimate persuasion.

Most of us will not minister with confidence and skill in the early stages of caring for souls. We need to hear, "You're on the right track" or "Here's how your situation might work better." The process of getting help with your personal ministry as leader can be called coaching. Sometimes it's one-on-one. Other times it occurs as you huddle with other leaders who are in the same role as you. Those who can thrive without much coaching, encouragement, and supervision are in the minority.

Regular, quality supervision can compensate for lack of extensive training.

Many small group leaders invite their coach to their meetings for first-hand observation and feedback. What better opportunity to gain a firsthand view of the kinds of ministry challenges you're facing? Then, when you receive feedback, your growth as a leader can accelerate.

If you're a group leader, then you have every reason to expect that your church will arrange its staff and resources in a way that supports you. Your senior pastor needs to connect you with someone in authority so that you can feel your ministry is making a legitimate contribution to the work of the church.

Understanding Authority Leads to God's Blessing

Matthew 8:5-13 indicates how submission to authority contributed to faith. In your willingness to seek advice and to take correction and input, you'll be like that Roman officer who came to Jesus with a sick servant. He said, in effect, "I'm a man under authority and I have people under authority who serve me. I understand the nature of authority. I have come to believe that my servant's sickness is under your authority, Jesus. Would you please order his sickness to depart?"

Jesus responded with a powerful observation; that He hadn't found faith like that in the whole nation of Israel. "Then Jesus said to the centurion, 'Go! It will be done just as you believed it would.' And his servant was healed at that very hour" (Matthew 8:13).

This Roman officer was a middle manager. He reported to those over him in a military hierarchy. Because of his position, he was also in charge of people who worked under his direction. He exercised authority which came by virtue of his cooperating with those over him.

This centurion seemed to recognize a hierarchy in which Jesus exercised God's power over sickness, which was within Jesus' authority to order about. His faith consisted of recognizing Jesus' authority and led to great benefit to his household. As today's teenagers say, the religious leaders "just didn't get it." The religious leaders were clueless while the Roman military "got it."

Although the analogy has been and can be abused, your pastor and other elders stand in the position of undershepherds to Christ (see 1 Peter 5:2). They oversee the spiritual welfare of your congregation. If you are closely collaborating with them, your ministry will be enhanced by its being perceived as an extension of their spiritual authority.

As you create a following and resolve to be a spiritual blessing to each life within your influence, be a person who can be coached. Seek a ministry supervisor who will listen to your report and mentor you.

You will have taken an important step of empowerment for effective ministry.

RECRUIT

Connect: Build a strong link with the pastoral staff.

 Recruit: Keep your leadership nucleus fresh and growing.

Invite:

Prepare:

Meet:

Bring:

Serve:

Win:

Seek:

CHAPTER

5

🔑 KEY TWO:
RECRUIT A LEADER-IN-TRAINING

CHAPTER SUMMARY

How to Recruit:
1. Commit yourself to being a leader who produces other group leaders.
2. Recruit apprentices who are willing to serve as leaders-in-training.
3. Use spiritual-gift identification to draw untapped talent into leadership training roles.
4. Train your apprentice by modeling and feedback.
5. Make sure your apprentice has access to training beyond what you can provide.

YOU AND I HAVE BEEN LEFT IN THIS WORLD BECAUSE GOD'S not finished with it yet. We're still here because God is interested in bringing people into His love and family. As long as there are still people He's calling to enter His family, we will have a job to do. If we are effective in being part of what God is doing, the church will experience growing pains.

Acts 6:1-7 reports that as the early church grew, it faced a reminder of these truths. No longer was it possible or advisable for the apostles to make enough bread runs to feed all the widows. Despite their best efforts, these sincere, busy, spiritual leaders were faulted for missing people. Tension rose as the neglected widows complained. Church leaders had to make a decision.

The apostles could have responded by launching a sermon series entitled, "Don't Gripe." Instead they said, in effect, "We need to identify additional leaders who can help us shoulder this load, so that we can expand the ministry in the part of the church that's growing the fastest among the Greek-speaking Jews." Being Hebrews themselves, the apostles perhaps didn't have a strong communication line with the Greek-speaking wing of the church. Their solution was to approve seven new leaders, whose Greek names suggest that they knew how to connect with the Greek-speaking widows. By filling that need, the church was able to find peace and go forward from there.

It seems that the new life God brought into the church had gotten ahead of its ability to ensure quality caregiving. The fellowship of the church couldn't be expanded until new workers were released into ministry.

The fellowship of the church couldn't be expanded until new workers were released into ministry.

Likewise today the harvest God gives a congregation sometimes gets ahead of its leadership development. Then the momentum slows down, plateaus, or even goes into decline because of the dissatisfaction that comes from people's needs not being met.

If the New Testament solution was to expand the care capacity of the church by raising up new leaders, then it's reasonable for congregations today to ask the same underlying question: "Why leave leadership development to chance?" Just as the typical church is intentional about its preaching, worship, prayer life, and other core values of the faith, why not be systematic about leadership development as well?

The New Testament solution was to expand the base of the church by raising up new leaders.

View Yourself as a Leader Maker—and Your Group as a Leader-Making Laboratory

Apprenticing is a Biblical way of life. Joshua was tutored by Moses. Elisha was brought on by Elijah. The Apostles were recruited and trained by Jesus. Timothy was mentored by Paul who, in turn, was discipled by Barnabas.

How to Recruit #1: Commit yourself to being a leader who produces other group leaders.

One of the clearest patterns of apprenticeship through groups appears in Paul's instruction to Timothy: "The things you have heard me say in the presence of many witnesses entrust to reliable men who will also be qualified to teach others" (2 Timothy 2:2). This verse alone covers four generations of worker multiplication: (1) Paul with others, (2) to Timothy and company, (3) to other reliable leaders, (4) and then onward to still others.

Sometimes the apprentice surpasses the mentor. For example, shortly after Paul's conversion, a leader of the Jerusalem church named Barnabas befriended and discipled him. In time the two men ministered side by side. Then a transition occurred as "Barnabas and Paul" became "Paul and Barnabas" (see Acts 4:36-37, 9:26-28, 11:19-30, 13:1-13, 15:1-4, 35). The final New Testament reference to Barnabas depicts him as apparently restarting the pattern by taking Mark under his wing (Acts 15:36-41).

The idea of a mentored leadership team seems to be central to most of the role models throughout Scripture. This repetition and centrality suggest that the creation of pastoral, ministry-capable leadership must become the core value of the church of the future, second only to listening to God in prayer.

> **The creation of pastoral, ministry-capable leadership must become the core value of the church of the future, second only to listening to God in prayer.**

The central leadership task of the church, after hearing from God, is to develop leaders—leaders for care-centered evangelistic cells; leaders who produce various large-group events; leaders who produce church-wide worship celebrations; leaders who organize and carry out all the ministries given by God to a congregation.

> **The central leadership task of the church, after hearing from God, is to develop leaders.**

After all, the assignment of the Christian church is not preaching as an end in itself. According to the Great Commission as recorded in Matthew 28:19-20, our task is to create obedient disciples of Jesus Christ. We are not to be so much a pulpit-focused spectatorship as a disciple-producing movement. Two thousand years of history demonstrate that the churches which have made a difference got people together in groups of about a dozen or less and held them accountable to obey the Word of God—not just to listen to it.

> **Churches which have made a difference got people together in groups ...and held them accountable to obey the Word of God.**

❦

We are not to be so much a pulpit-focused spectatorship as a disciple-producing movement.

❦

Be on a Constant Talent Search

How, then, can you be a strategic part of what God is doing to redeem a sinful world? You start by recruiting and training your own replacement as a leader. This is not a control or ownership issue, but a matter of steward-ship. You don't own the group who may call you its leader. Rather, from a leadership development standpoint, the group you serve—whether called a class, team, board, Bible study, or whatever— is a teaching hospital, a manifestation of the Body of Christ for training the next generation of volunteer workers.

How to Recruit #2: Recruit apprentices who are willing to serve as leaders-in-training.

❦

From a leadership development standpoint, the group ...is a laboratory ...for training the next generation of volunteer workers.

❦

Churches around the continent employ a variety of terms to describe the apprentice role. Perhaps the most popular expressions are *apprentice, intern,* and *leader-in-training.* I've also run across the terms *understudy, mentor partner, co-leader, student leader, helper, junior leader,* and *assistant leader.*

Whatever labels you use, beware of a common pitfall as you build your leadership nucleus: Make sure that those you are mentoring understand the distinction between an assistant and an apprentice. Your assistant will help you carry a log. An apprentice will learn how to carry the log, and will eventually take it away with a helper of his or her own. There's a world of difference between these two roles.

Your assistant will help you carry a log. An apprentice will learn how to carry the log, and will eventually take it away with a helper of his or her own.

Most people who volunteer for the role of assistant see their primary responsibility as helping you succeed. In many cases, such people take on the role of host or hostess, coordinating food for the snack time. Or perhaps they line up babysitting for the infant children of group members. Or maybe they take care of the meeting location, making sure that a home, classroom, or restaurant side room is available each time the group gathers.

The assistant role is vital, enabling you to focus on the people development. If you try to do it yourself, you will burn out from trying to wear too many hats. Or you'll be so consumed with venue, childcare, and other arrangements that you won't have time for your more strategic pastoral role.

Therefore, make much of prayer as you begin to build a leadership nucleus. In most cases, you'll want at least two people in the nucleus in addition to yourself. Each will demonstrate a differing aspiration, with gifts appropriate to those roles. (For churchwide help in identifying a pool of potential leaders see the "Find X Survey" in Appendix B).

Suppose you develop a sidekick whose gift of helps provides a motivation to assist you. You may both have a wonderful time, but that relationship may be a dead-end street in terms of passing the baton. That individual would probably be best thought of as an assistant, not an apprentice.

Apprentices come to the group with an entirely different agenda. They will become leaders in their own right because they have been mentored by you. They will develop a two-aspect vision of what God can accomplish through the group. They will see the group as a place of one-another ministry designed to encourage all the people in the group. And they also will view the group as a training forum for the leadership nucleus.

As you develop your apprentices, you are always working two levels deep. You need an apprentice, and your apprentice needs an apprentice. That is because you can't promote your apprentice unless you have a replacement apprentice identified for each of you. So you're continually seeking to work with three people: one apprentice and two rising apprentices. You're not leading at a level capable of reproducing yourself until you are leading others who are leading others.

You're continually seeking to work with three people: one apprentice and two rising apprentices.

Be a Leader Who Produces Other Group Leaders

Once in a while a small-group leader reacts negatively to this train-a-replacement approach. The reasoning goes like this: "Why would I want to give away the ministry that I enjoy doing so very much?" Often, upon probing, it turns out that such a person thinks in terms of "holding a good meeting equals maximum-impact ministry."

Is that equation an adequate definition of ministry? It won't hold up if God is calling your church to expand its network of care. Until every current leader in your church becomes a leader-maker, you will never begin to develop the numbers of leaders needed to have a healthy, growing church. Tomorrow's leaders with a bias toward evangelism need to think of themselves as leader-makers as well as group conveners.

Tomorrow's leaders ...need to think of themselves as leader-makers as well as group conveners.

From the point of view of a church's overall strategy, it makes all the sense in the world for every leader to think of training one or more successors. In this fashion a church's leadership base begins to expand without taxing the resources of the staff. If a church stays focused on this leader-finding approach, 80% to 95% of the new leaders it needs can be discovered by its existing leaders.

When a church decentralizes the ministry of leader development in this fashion, it can follow suit with other elements of administration as well. For example, in many churches every group takes responsibility for its own childcare. Groups then have far more options for when to meet, where to meet, and how to address the spiritual needs of their youngsters once they're no longer restricted to Wednesday nights, 7:00-9:00, in order to coincide with the staff-run children's programs and nursery.

Mobilize People by Spiritual-Gift Identification

How to Recruit #3: Use spiritual-gift identification to draw untapped talent into leadership-training roles.

One of the most effective tools you have for bringing people into candidacy for group leadership is to start affirming their spiritual gifts. How? Study what the Bible says about various spiritual gifts. Become acquainted with how lay-mobilization books and programs interpret the relevant Scriptures (see Appendix C for a partial listing of such resources). Then watch how people minister to one another in your group.

One of the most effective tools you have for bringing people into candidacy for group leadership is to start affirming their spiritual gifts.

When in a small-group setting, Christians intuitively minister out of God's grace through their spiritual gift or gifts. In an auditorium venue, where lots of people sit somewhat passively, listening to a teacher, you rarely see different people's spiritual gifts at work.

However, try putting those same listeners in contact with real need—Person A's teen is acting up, Person B has a personality conflict with the boss at work, or Person C's bills can't be paid out of current resources. If you watch several individuals interact to support one another, you'll realize that not everyone acts alike in offering help. That difference in action is a consequence of the Holy Spirit's activity.

In a small-group setting, Christians intuitively minister out of God's grace through their spiritual gift or gifts.

In the group you serve, whenever you catch Christians doing good, it's probably because they're using their spiritual gifts. Affirm them. Raise their consciousness about the possibility that their fruitfulness and joy could be an evidence of the Holy Spirit's work in their life.

Suppose you say to someone, "I get so much comfort when I talk to you; the things you say bring such peace to me. I can really see God at work. I think maybe the Holy Spirit has given you the gift of comforter."

Don't be surprised if you hear a somewhat bewildered reply: "What? All I'm doing is being myself with you." Most people are so unaware of the unique and special work of God in their lives that they sometimes can't see it, except through the reflected appraisals of affirming people.

To another person you'll say, "I need some advice and counsel on a sticky situation. Every time I've talked to you, I've carried away wisdom and it's been a huge help to me. I think God must have given you the gift of wisdom because when you offer me guidance, it works."

Then later at that person's home: "Honey, Marjorie tonight said that every time she gets my advice, it works. She's come to rely on that."

"That's right. Everybody knows that except you."

As people are affirmed for their gifts, they come to realize that they are responsible for the stewardship of that gift. Every spiritual gift is given by the Holy Spirit for a reason. The purpose is to

51

enable Christians to encourage or build up other members of the Body of Christ and to draw in those who are outside the Body (see Romans 12, 1 Corinthians 12-14).

As people are affirmed for their gifts, they come to realize that they are responsible for the stewardship of that gift.

Avoid Patterns that Lead to Burnout

In tapping into people's gifts, you're not trying to impose additional burdens, but to surface gifted leaders. If you want people to be resistant to burnout, get them involved in ministry that's consistent with their gifts. Don't ask, "What slots can they fill in our programs?" or "What can these people do for us?" Rather, focus on "What can this church do to make it possible for these leaders to use their God-given gift?"

People will burn out if they're not supervised, appreciated, or kept from being stretched too thin. The most durable people are the ones who discover and use the gifts God has given them for ministry.

People who are encouraged to use their giftedness report new energy and joy in using them. They benefit from the exercise at the same time others are blessed by it.

Lead Your Apprentice and Group into Gift Maturity

If your foot hurts, you don't go to a dentist. If your ear hurts, you don't go to a physical therapist. When you have a cold, you don't go to a podiatrist. All of these people may be healthcare professionals, but each represents only one part of an entire community of skills. If you say, "I need healthcare," you then must choose between surgeons, podiatrists, allergists, and dozens of other areas of specialty.

Likewise the Holy Spirit has provided for the spiritual health and growth of the church by giving a whole variety of abilities to different members of the body. He distributed His gifts in order to cause Christians to appreciate one another and to work interdependently. The way we learn to love and respect one another is to recognize the uniqueness of how God has made each individual. We each provide something that other people need.

The Holy Spirit ...distributed His gifts in order to cause Christians to appreciate one another and to work interdependently.

The more mature you become, the more you rely on the work of God through other believers. You begin to rely on the wisdom of one person, the comfort of another person, the guidance or exhortation of still another. It may be a highly spiritual act to approach a fellow group member and say, "I think I need a swift kick and I've learned that I can count on you to know what to do next."

The more mature you become, the more you rely on the work of God through other believers.

At one particular crossroad in my own life, God gave me an exhorter who asked the questions that led me to the career I've been in for almost two decades now. A mercy-gifted person might have said, "I can sense that this is a very perplexing time for you." A teacher would have approached my situation at another level, perhaps inquiring, "What do you think God is trying to teach you?" But the exhorter knew how to take me through my pain to a new objective by asking, "If you were to use the gifts the Holy Spirit has given you, what would you be doing?" When you are part of a community of faith, God will give each person to you that you need.

When you are part of a community of faith, God will give each person to you that you need.

53

If you and all other current leaders in your church begin to be aware of the fact that there is someone nearby who is capable of taking your job, then you're close to where you need to be for church-transforming gift discovery. People who are the gifts of God to the Body of Christ may not be aware of it. Your task is to discover at least one of these gifted people–to recruit your replacement.

Know Where to Look for New Apprentices

Why don't churches have enough leaders? The answer usually has nothing to do with inadequacy on the part of your present cadre of elected or appointed leaders. Instead I have yet to find a case where the number of potential but unrecognized leaders is not at least equal to the number of existing, identified leaders.

I have yet to find a case where the number of potential but unrecognized leaders is not at least equal to the number of existing, identified leaders.

The typical church involves about 10% of its people in public leadership roles. They usually constitute the talent pool for electable office or appointment—the highly visible places of congregational leadership. People who are acknowledged to be the stuff of which leaders are made generally comprise an overworked minority. They're your base of core people who chair the board, superintend the Sunday school, become elected as a deacon, or volunteer to chair the property-evaluation committee.

The good news is that there is another undiscovered group that has not been tapped into because its "members" don't have a desire or need to put themselves forward by nominating themselves for leadership. They have the intelligence, character, heart, gifts, and ability to be effective leaders if invited to do so; but they usually won't offer themselves. If you approach them on a one-on-one basis with, "I believe you could do this," they hesitantly say, "I could? I'm willing to give it a try if you think I could handle it." They are discovered leaders, not self-named leaders.

How do you spot them? In order to invite them to a leadership role that you can confer upon them, you must know them personally. Since they're generally not the type to put themselves forward, then the main way you'll notice is if you are in close proximity. If you get them in a group of 5 to 10 people, they don't stay hidden; it becomes obvious that they're desirable persons to become leaders. That's the context in which this second group of leaders comes out of the woodwork; they can't hide their leadership ability. That's why it is helpful to develop a practice of apprenticing at the small-group level.

If you get them in a group of 5 to 10 people, they don't stay hidden; it becomes obvious that they're desirable persons to become leaders.

When I begin talking with pastors or boards about developing a small-group network of meaningful caregivers, they often think through the labor-intensive implications of the personnel that will be required. Then they ask, "Where are we going to find the people? Our officers are overworked and overextended already. They can't carve out more time."

The good news is that there is an invisible layer of untapped talent in almost every congregation. Typically there is another 10% who are not being called upon to be leaders. Why? This segment is largely undeveloped because it doesn't put itself forward. People like this usually don't volunteer themselves for ministry; instead they have to be invited.

There is an invisible layer of untapped talent in almost every congregation.

Church after church is tapping into a whole new layer of lay ability, doubling the size of the church leadership with people who are ministry capable at the level of the cell, whether or not they are electable to other offices. One of the most important roles of the coach (introduced in the previous chapter) is to help small group leaders identify potential apprentices from that "secretly warehoused" talent pool.

Your job as a small-group leader is to learn how to replace yourself with a ministry-capable apprentice. You're not promotable to a new field of ministry until you have your replacement in sight and functioning well. More important, newcomers can't receive the intimate care of a small group unless enough leaders are available to convene those groups. The idea of bringing new people alongside yourself through apprenticeship is a way to assure the church that it has the leaders needed for the future.

Newcomers can't receive the intimate care of a small group unless enough leaders are available to convene those groups.

You can confidently predict that every year your church develops a net of 10 new ministry-capable leaders with apprentices, you could add 100 people to your attendance. In other words, your role in leadership development can help enlarge your church's network of care.

Every year your church develops ...10 new ministry-capable leaders with apprentices, you could add 100 people to your attendance.

That network will result in a larger worship attendance. I've seen these numbers work in churches with a worship attendance of 100, of 1,000, of 10,000, and even in the overseas churches with attendances exceeding 100,000. In time, your overall worship attendance will grow to the number of new leaders you develop times ten.

If you believe God is calling you to build a numerically growing church, the first step is to set goals for developing new leaders, knowing that one of the consequences is an expanding base of ministry. A leader based, small group growth approach, whether Sunday school class or home-based care group, grows around units of 10. Thus the quality of that church's care level never needs to be diminished by the arrival of new converts. No matter how many new believers God gives you, they're cared for one at a time in the context of 10. The care standard remains constant, whatever the overall size the church becomes.

The quality of that church's care level never needs to be diminished by the onset of new converts.

With a span of care that small, people can feel so loved that they don't want to leave. Paid staff can provide a 1:10 care level to at most a handful of groups. (By comparison, a church staff member, devoting full time to leadership development and working with a network of coaches, can sustain about 50 cells, especially as these cells learn to feed their own growth because they are developing enough leaders). However, if you're constantly developing new leaders, you can afford to lavish that 1:10 level of care. Enough believers in enough groups will receive enough gifts of the Holy Spirit to enable the church to have a never ending supply of leaders.

Enough believers in enough groups will receive enough gifts of the Holy Spirit to enable the church to have a never ending supply of leaders.

In our churches there's never been a greater need for caring leaders than we face today. The needs of the family and community are so great that a church can put every leader to work, especially because the idea is not for the church staff to create groups which they hand to leaders, but to cultivate leaders who can develop a following. Any leaders of this type who don't have a group grow a new one. Thus, however many leaders you can develop, you can have that many cells and classes. The birthing of new groups is not based on group division so much as on leadership multiplication. You don't create goals for new groups so much as you cultivate new leaders.

In our churches there's never been a greater need for caring leaders than we face today.

The birthing of new groups is not based on group division so much as on leadership multiplication.

Once Found, Ease New Leaders into the Apprentice Role

Are you starting a new group? As you begin your journey, start by picking out two or more people who will form your leadership nucleus. Do this even before you decide who to invite as members of the group. In fact, many churches don't let leaders call meetings of a newly formed group until they've built their nucleus. One reason for this goal is so that your apprentice(s) and assistant(s) can work with you in the recruitment part of the process. As a result, you are placing your leader-in-training in a leadership role from the very beginning.

How to Recruit #4: Train your apprentice by modeling and feedback.

Has your church ever had a recognized network of small groups? When you're first starting small groups in a church, you may need to prayerfully discover people who have previously made the commitment to empowered ministry through groups. Often a church will take a survey and find out who has led small groups. There's a lot of underutilized talent who have already developed group leadership skills from attending previous churches.

Once identified, invite these experienced people to be the initial wave of small group leaders. Early on, insist on their recruiting an apprentice. From that point on they can be championed as leader-producers. After each leader is in place and has recruited an apprentice, then there is double energy at work in talent-search mode.

Or are you serving a pre-existing group or pre-existing system in which you are first introducing the apprentice concept? Having prayerfully identified someone as a potential leader, offer an assignment that represents something an apprentice would do. Over time, your rising apprentice will conclude, "I have no real excuse for not moving forward. I can accept more responsibility in this area."

I remember being in a group with a young man who was extremely talented, but somewhat unsure of himself. He was the kind of person who panicked at the thought of public speaking. I was testing him out as a potential apprentice, so I asked if he would lead the Bible study portion the next week.

His first reaction was to recoil in terror. "I couldn't do that," he said. "What would they think?"

"Who do you mean by *they*?" I asked.

"Everybody, you know," he replied.

"Well, you speak to them every week as a participant in the group," I pointed out.

"I've never thought of myself as a leader," he said. "But if it's just us, then sure." Over several weeks he overcame his limited self-perception and matured into an excellent group leader. It took almost all of us in the group to keep affirming him until he truly believed he could do an able job of leading.

Don't Limit Apprenticeship to Meeting Times

In order to train someone to do what you do, you need to give your apprentice a leadership role both *in* every meeting and *between* every meeting. During the meetings the apprentice might handle the greeting, oversee a prayer time, lead a Bible study, facilitate a planning time, or look with you for new talent. Between meetings, apprentices can help with such leadership matters as praying, debriefing, phoning, arranging childcare, contacting prospects, ensuring follow-up on a care need, phoning unusually quiet group members or those who were criticized during the meeting, or contacting absentees.

You need to give your apprentice a leadership role both *in* every meeting and *between* every meeting.

By sharing the ministry in this way, you can systematically exercise your apprentice in various areas. If you are ill or out of town one week, your apprentice may carry an entire meeting without you. Soon enough you can both look back over the last three to six months, realizing that everything called for on the part of a leader has been covered at least two to three times.

Between meetings, apprentices can help with...
- **praying,**
- **debriefing,**
- **phoning,**
- **arranging childcare,**
- **contacting prospects,**
- **ensuring follow-up on a care need,**
- **phoning unusually quiet group members, or**
- **contacting absentees.**

As you ease your apprentice into leadership responsibilities, place just as much emphasis, if not more, on the facets of group life that occur outside the meeting. Remember that the secret of a group's vitality is found *between* the meetings as much as *in* the meeting.

The secret of a group's vitality is found *between* the meetings as much as *in* the meeting.

Some groups will have both assistant leaders and apprentice leaders. The "assistant" label tends to appeal to those with the gift of helps. The question that often works best with an assistant is, "Would you help me?" However, the apprentice may respond better to, "Can I stretch you a bit by trying something new?" Generally the assistant and the apprentice are willing to accept the same kinds of assignments–making calls, leading in prayer, following-up on an absentee–though perhaps the assistant more on a case-by-case level and the apprentice more on an ongoing level. Often the assistant, after trying on the apprentice garb in piecemeal fashion, may later express a willingness to become an apprentice.

Modeling and Feedback Are Indispensable

Gift-aware people know that God expects them to use their gifts in the building of the body. As you apprentice someone, remember that a person's motivation in ministry usually stems from spiritual-gifts issues. Paul told Timothy, probably referring to spiritual gifts, "Do not neglect your gift..." (1 Timothy 4:14). Similarly, if your apprentice's endowments from the Holy Spirit go unused, your training will miss a crucial ingredient.

How does an apprentice learn best? On-the-job training works best through a combination of joining you in action and receiving behind-the-scenes debriefing in the process. Here's how the sequence works:

1. I do, you watch, we talk.
2. I do, you help, we talk.
3. You do, I help, we talk.
4. You do, I watch, we talk.
5. We each begin to train someone else. Depending on our new roles and the coaching relationship we may have developed,

61

perhaps we continue dialoging together about our groups.

The process begins as you bring an apprentice closely enough alongside you to be able to watch you work. Then you let your apprentice help you. Next the apprentice tries it while you watch. Finally, you not only step aside and watch your apprentice at work, but also you stay nearby until your apprentice is apprenticing someone else. As a result, the leadership pool in your church will be ever widening.

You stay nearby until your apprentice is apprenticing someone else.

What do you want your apprentice to learn? Actually, once your coach gets you into a positive, forward-looking mode of shaping the future by setting new goals, you'll find it relatively easy to copycat that technique with your apprentice. You wind up aiding your apprentice the same way you're being helped by your coach (described in the previous chapter of this book).

Let's look at an actual example from a home group. We join the leader and apprentice as they debrief the most recent meeting. The blockage the leader and apprentice are facing is an overly talkative person. To compound the problem, the leader's personality is not the kind where confrontation and assertion come naturally.

Notice how the leader, almost without realizing it, copies problem-solving skills learned from the coach's modeling. Notice also the spiritual gifts each person uses and how they, as presents from God, are a great help in the problem solving. Perhaps the leader is a mercy type, and the apprentice an exhorter type (see Romans 12:8).

APPRENTICE: "...I agree, it was another great evening. I think it's because you and I pray for each person who comes. There was one thing about the meeting that bothered me, though. Joey runs his mouth the whole time. He had something to say about everybody's contribution. He's offending a number of the people in the group."

LEADER: "You're right, but I don't know how to get him to talk less."

APPRENTICE: "Just tell him to shut up."

LEADER: "I can't do that; not in those words, and not in the meeting."

APPRENTICE: "Then get Bob. He has the strongest personality in our group."

LEADER: "He'll scream, "JOEY, SHUT UP," and neither one will be back to the next group meeting. Or they'll duke it out as they walk to their cars."

APPRENTICE: "Well somebody's got to be responsible for controlling Joey. Too bad he's not dating anybody right now."

LEADER: "Joey ought to be able to control himself, but it's not working. That switch is missing at this point in his life."

APPRENTICE: "I know, our coach can visit the group, take Joey off to the side and say, 'You've got to help us here by listening more and talking less.'"

LEADER: "Maybe that's a good second line of defense, but I somehow think we're responsible to try first, like Matthew 18:15-17 teaches. Our coach keeps telling us not to act like we're helpless. I already hear the question coming, 'What are *you* going to do about Joey?' Our job as leaders includes being responsible to maintain the tone of the meeting."

APPRENTICE: "Okay, then why don't we pretend like I'm Joey?"

LEADER: "Well, it can't be during the group meeting. If I spoke to him then, I'd scare others. They might think I'll treat them as roughly as I'm treating Joey."

APPRENTICE: "Okay, pretend you've called me on the phone: 'Joey here. How can I help you?'"

LEADER: "This is a stretching experience for me. I've never confronted so directly before. I appreciate your help by role playing."

APPRENTICE: "Hey, I've got the easy part. 'Joey here again. How can I help you?'"

LEADER: "I like the way our coach always sincerely builds me up, so I'll start that way. Here goes. 'Joey, I need your help. What you had to say this week had some really profound insights. I can hardly wait until you have developed into a group leader.'"

APPRENTICE: "Thanks. What do you need me to do?"

LEADER: "I want you to help me develop the rest of the group so that they can talk as well as you can."

APPRENTICE: "Great. What should I do?"

LEADER: "When I say, 'Joey, let's talk about that afterwards,' that's your cue to let someone else talk. Don't say anything for at least five minutes. Will you make that deal with me?"

APPRENTICE: "How would that help? I talk most when you don't get the points straight and you need me to correct them."

LEADER: "Joey, I learn a lot from you, I really do. But I want to learn from others, too."

APPRENTICE: "What would they have to say that's important? They don't know the Bible like you and I do."

LEADER: "Joey, awhile back Pastor asked all of us leaders to read a book. It taught us that listening is a key to leadership in a small group. How well you listen is far more important than how well you talk. Joey, you'll learn to be a better leader if you make that deal with me."

APPRENTICE: "Okay, I'm taking my 'Joey' hat off. I'm me again. That was really good!"

LEADER: "That dialog pushed me way beyond my comfort zone. Maybe my real blockage is not Joey, but the fact that I'm still learning when to be assertive."

APPRENTICE: "Well, you showed Joey that you care. You were far more tactful than I'd be. What's the worst that can happen? Joey gets his feelings hurt, blows up, and goes to another church."

LEADER: "I hope not. I simply want to tell Joey that we can't give people a chance to be listened to if he's talking so much."

APPRENTICE: "If he continues to talk, that's when we bring the coach in to help us find another strategy."

LEADER: "Right. Just before I phone Joey, maybe tomorrow, can I call you for prayer and moral support?"

APPRENTICE: "Sure, just let your fingers do the walking."

The goal and value of peer counseling, as illustrated in the dialog above, can take care of 95% (if not more) of the problems group leaders deal with. It's usually not a complicated matter that thwarts a ministry. In this case the leader, perhaps a bit codependent in personality, needed to learn not to feel helpless. Prayerful interaction with the apprentice and role modeling from the coach led to an idea for how to control Joey's offensive behavior.

Peer counseling ...can take care of 95% (if not more) of the problems group leaders deal with.

The word *edification*, when defined by Bible scholars, seems similar in meaning to this peer counseling idea. In both cases one person builds another up, helping solve problems through skills like active listening, empathizing with people's feelings, offering correction, and laying out a course of action. If we practice the "one anothers" of Scripture on each other (listed in Key Five), we'll be doing a lot of peer counseling. If we use spiritual gifts of exhortation, helps, teaching, pastoring, and mercy giving, among others, we'll again be doing a lot of peer counseling. The sequence also works in reverse: peer counseling leads to increased spiritual gift usage and one-another ministry.

Apprentices Need to Be Constant Learners

What about the remaining 5% or so of problems—the ones that don't seem to be solved by peer counseling? Together with your apprentice, ask for help from the person serving as your coach. Also present the issue to other ministry leaders at your church. These counselors may not give you an answer you expect. They may refer you to everything from a season of fasting to a seminar or book. In

How to Recruit #5: Make sure your apprentice has access to training beyond what you can provide.

65

most cases, however, the wisdom you need will come as you ask, seek, and knock (see Matthew 7:7-8).

Finally, what about discipleship; how does it occur in cells? The primary focus of discipleship takes place in the leadership nucleus. Discipleship best occurs through the process of cultivating apprentices. In other words, discipleship comes not so much from exhorting the group as a whole as from helping apprentices become full-fledged leaders and then assisting these new, rising leaders to find their own apprentices. In a growing cell, this leadership hub can represent 40% of the cells' membership.

Discipleship best occurs through the process of cultivating apprentices.

Thus discipleship in small groups comes not so much from urging the whole group as from cultivating apprentices. It will, of course, also occur on a lesser and more casual level, as members interact one with another.

Release New Groups without Unnecessary Ripples

As a group welcomes and assimilates new members, leaders and members alike become concerned about its increasing size. If it becomes too big, it will lose the very feature that drew many people to it: the smallness, intimacy, and ability to listen to everyone involved.

If you try to split a group (even if you use words like *multiply* or *birth*), people will often fight you, call you names, give you grief, and resent you. Why? Because most humans resist change, especially if they've finally found something they like. However, if you have leaders who lead some of the members out into new groups, the members will often say, "Isn't this fun?"

The point of change is the apprenticing process, not the splitting of groups.

The reasoning works like this. When you as a leader focus on birthing, it's hard to manage because you're dealing with the entire group. Instead, focus on the leadership nucleus, and the role of the apprentice leader in particular. Birthing then becomes one of the consequences of handling the apprentice-development process well. The leadership nucleus is where leadership multiplication issues are dealt with.

Birthing then becomes one of the consequences of handling the apprentice-development process well.

Growing groups will tend to birth, some in 6 months, but most will take longer. The norm is a year or two. More often than not, it's the leader who moves out to start a new group, leaving the apprentice behind. The leader and former apprentice don't need to say good-bye to each other because they enter a new level of fellowship at the huddle level as they are coached (see Key Two for comments on the "huddle" concept).

The leader and former apprentice don't need to say good-bye to each other because they enter a new level of fellowship at the huddle level as they are coached.

It's not even the closed-group or open-group dimension that makes the difference in whether group multiplication occurs; it's whether an apprentice leader is present. You can have a group that's closed but develops an apprentice and then supports that apprentice in assuming leadership of the current group or in departing to start a new group.

Group multiplication will become inevitable as the pastoral leadership in your church deputizes each current leader into a committee-of-one designed to recruit and train a new leader during the next 6 to 12 months. Currently, only about 4% of the workers in a typical church are focused on the leader-finding task. That would include nominating committees, Sunday school superintendents, and some or all of the pastoral staff. If encouraged to do so, however, some 80% of your existing leaders will be easily able to find people to come alongside them. The remaining 20% need the help of the pastoral staff to find an apprentice.

Only about 4% of the workers in a typical church are focused on the leader-finding task.

Churches across North America are discovering a whole new generation of previously-hidden leaders. This breakthrough means that your church, if focused on developing leaders for Jesus Christ, is headed for a transformation.

If every current leader in your church becomes a leader-maker, you will begin to develop the numbers of leaders needed to have an adequately functioning church. You can't afford to miss any opportunity to develop new leaders because the best place to develop a new leader is at the elbow of an existing leader—you!

If every current leader ...becomes a leader-maker, you will begin to develop the numbers of leaders needed to have an adequately functioning church.

INVITE

Connect: *Build a strong link with the pastoral staff.*

Recruit: *Keep your leadership nucleus fresh and growing.*

Invite: Cultivate a larger contact group through enthusiasm and care.

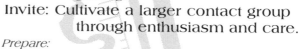

Prepare:

Meet:

Bring:

Serve:

Win:

Seek:

70

6

CHAPTER

KEY THREE:
INVITE NEWCOMERS TO
YOUR GROUP

CHAPTER SUMMARY

How to Invite:
☑ 1. Meet with your leadership nucleus.
☑ 2. Understand the mathematics of invitation.
☑ 3. Create a contact list.
☑ 4. Prioritize the contact list.
☑ 5. Be warm and enthusiastic.

JULIA CHILD, GRAHAM KERR, AND JEFF SMITH HAVE EACH RE-
ceived worldwide acclaim for their cooking abilities. These gifted
chefs can assemble beautiful and tasteful meals from all kinds of
foods. They dice this, mix in that, baste lightly, simmer briefly, add
one more ingredient, and voilà–another winning combination. These
culinary experts use various pots, pans, and utensils in the process, but
the cookware is not the focus; the food is.

Your small group meeting can be compared to a pot. It's a "container"

71

that holds people next to each other for a while. When everyone is together, the Holy Spirit uses the closeness to do some work. The relationships that form within the context of that "pot" are what count. The pot itself is merely a tool for two dynamics to occur. First, it enables everyone gathered to encourage one another. Second, it gives a leader a chance to show an apprentice how to facilitate a meeting.

In the all-important process of making disciples, one of the most strategic utensils is the small group. The "cookware" may come in different brands and shapes, according to the kind of "dish" desired. Similarly the type of group may also vary, such as with a care circle, ministry team, covenant group, or small Sunday school class. Whatever its name and specific function, at a foundational level each group is also a place where relationships are formed. The Holy Spirit works as people listen to and care for each other, "speaking the truth in love" (Ephesians 4:15).

Leaders Can Model Base Community

My point is this: Your small group, whatever its announced objective, will be more effective if members make time to offer pastoral care to

How to Invite #1: Meet with your leadership nucleus.

one another. A drama team will often perform better if members make time for mutual nurture. A Sunday school class will bond more closely when its participants make time to address personal needs. An usher corps will be friendlier when its members connect emotionally with each other, whether through a quick pre-service huddle or an occasional home-based evening of desserts.

Therefore, as you prepare to invite people to your group, you will find that the best way to begin is in community as you call together a leadership nucleus: you, an apprentice, and host or hostess. As the three or so of you meet, interact, and pray together, you will set the tone for the "one anothers" of Scripture. You will lay the foundation for the base community into which you can invite others into your fellowship and the fellowship of Jesus Christ.

For these reasons, when you meet with your leadership nucleus, don't immediately jump into the task of deciding who to invite. Don't go directly into prayer about the invitation process.

• First be intentional about connecting spiritually with one another. "How are you?" "What has God been teaching you lately?" "Where have you seen Him at work in your life and world?" "What burdens can we bear for each other?" "What cares can we together cast upon the Lord?"

• Next perhaps review the specific purpose or covenant of your group: "Why are we forming (or continuing) this group?" "What do we believe God wants to accomplish through us?"

• Finally, now you are ready to ask yourselves about the important role of community: "How important is it for us as a leadership team to model the kinds of relationships we're developing?" Then, the more you experience genuine spiritual community together, rather than merely talk or dream of it, the more enthusiastic you will be about inviting the entire yet-to-be-formed group into this same sense of deep fellowship. Team building occurs both during meetings and as you encounter one another between meetings.

The more you experience genuine spiritual community together ...the more enthusiastic you will be about inviting the ...group into this same sense of deep fellowship.

Calculate the Number of Contacts Needed

It is also important, before you do the actual inviting, to understand certain principles of human conduct.

How to Invite #2: Understand the mathematics of invitation.

Researchers, both secular and church-based, suggest that small groups are most effective somewhere between 8, 10, or 12 people. A few authorities propose that groups start with as few as 4 people, and a handful of others suggest 17 or so as the largest possible "small" group. By and large, the consensus hovers around a gathering size of about 10.

Why does the literature suggest a group of about 10 as the optimal amount? At that range, the group dynamics make the meeting just big enough to hide a bit if you're too bruised to show it—with just 4 or 5 it's too small to hide. Yet 10 people makes a meeting small enough to provide the help you need—with 14, 15, or more there's not enough time for everyone to be listened to.

If your target is 10 people, then the next step is to calculate the number of contacts you need to cultivate. The general rule of thumb is this: Be in active communication with 20 to 30 prospective participants, and in all likelihood you will end up with 10 at a given meeting. (If your target size is larger or smaller, simply scale the ratio appropriately).

All 20 to 30 need to be viable as possible members at present or in the not-too-distant future. Generally these will be people who are somewhat interested, but who may need to decline due to limitations of work, travel, and health, as well as childcare issues. Unless the Lord compels you otherwise, don't include people in your prospect list who tell you "I have zero interest, thank you" or "We're moving to another state next week."

Remember, you are developing this contact base in cooperation with the rest of your leadership nucleus. For example, suppose you're going to aim at an initial size of 10 members, and your leadership nucleus numbers 3 people—you, an apprentice, and a host. If you each successfully bring two others, and then one of you stumbles on a tenth person, you're ready to go.

What if all 25 invitees show up for one of your meetings? Almost any group will swell in size from time to time. Be assured that participants can handle it on occasion, although the sense of intimacy will considerably lessen and the quality of caring will diminish.

Then you'll have an evening with terrible weather. Only 8 or 10 will make it. After the meeting, people will console you, as leader, on the "low" attendance. Yet on the doorstep someone else will say, "But you know, this is one of the best meetings we've had in months." What they're reflecting on is how the meeting allowed everyone to be heard without feeling rushed or crowded.

People feel loved and cared for when you have time to hear from their heart. You can't do that in a rush. You need time for all participants to say whatever they need to say.

People feel loved and cared for when you have time to hear from their heart.

That's why a recurring theme in every chapter of this book is that we must develop more leaders. Existing groups, as they grow to the point of bulging, sometimes send members home unlistened to. On-deck, available new leaders can create a new listening point by moving out and forming another group. In normal situations, a leadership nucleus looks for the group to start multiplying anytime they're above 10 regular participants in number or are regularly using breakout groups (threesomes, foursomes) during your meetings.

Time to Make a List

Now you are ready to prayerfully make a prospect list of 10, 20, or 30 people whom you can invite. As a leadership nucleus, ask God to lead you to a series of divine appointments through those you contact. Now think through any pre-set limiters, such as "this will be a women's group" or "this will be a young-adult group." Next,

How to Invite #3: Create a contact list.

write down the names of the people you think might be receptive to you and able to come.

Some churches have trained their people to accept a list of assigned people. Often those groups report low retention levels. Instead, the people who come at your invitation are more likely to be open to receiving care from you than those who are arbitrarily assigned to you.

People who come at your invitation are more likely to be open to receiving care from you than those who are arbitrarily assigned to you.

The reason is simple: people have preferences. You want to be with Person A more than Person B. You find Person A more approachable than Person C. You have more common interests with Person A than with Person D. The principle makes sense: if people self-select themselves as being candidates for your care, then the care junction is properly made.

Here's an example of how affinity-based selection works. When our children were smaller, we decided to buy them a Great Dane puppy. We drove to a breeder who had a reputation for finding outstanding matches between puppies and families. I asked him if he could find us a match and then let us be on our way.

"Sure," he replied, "but we need to chat a bit first."

I thought he wanted to educate us in the care and feeding of this particular breed. He politely answered our questions, but didn't seem to have an instructional agenda.

"Are you going to be able to give us a puppy soon, so we can head out?" I asked again. "We have quite a drive to return home."

"Soon," he said, but then resumed chatting about the weather and other pass-the-time topics.

Finally, he went out into the yard where our children had been playing with a whole litter of Great Danes. "This is your pup," he said, scooping one up. "She'll work out just fine for you."

I was confused. How did he know? I pressed him for an explanation.

"I didn't make the decision," he replied. "This pup picked out your children. She's been following them happily all over the yard."

Suddenly I understood. "It makes such sense," I thought. He had waited to see where the chemistry would develop. Over those few minutes, some of the puppies had developed a much stronger bonding with our children than did others.

The ideal is that everyone who is a leader has been somewhat self-selected by each participant or follower.

The same principle works among people. The ideal is that everyone who is a leader has been somewhat self-selected by each participant or follower. These people, if they stay with you any length of time, will accept ministry from you in an ever expanding number of areas.

In seminars I lead, I sometimes introduce a process that illustrates this principle. Several times during our sessions, I'll have people form groups of three or four. I'll give them a brief assignment that involves a degree of self disclosure: "What do you hope to learn at this conference?" or "What idea troubles you the most so far, and why?" During various exercises, I'll direct participants into several work groups to extend their acquaintance list.

After a while, I'll help them make something called a sociogram. I ask, "Of the various people you met today, who was the person you had the most energy for, who you'd enjoy being with again?" Most people can almost always name someone they find more interesting than the rest. If I put them together, they have energy to create a relationship.

That dynamic, called affinity matching, translates into an important small-group principle: It's far more effective to listen to how people feel about others than to assign them based on ZIP codes or alphabetical listings.

If you're a leader who has been handed a list of people assigned to you, realize that only a certain number will genuinely "click" with you. Whenever possible, view the computer-generated list as a fishing pool. After a couple of months, take the sheet back to the church office and say, "These people haven't shown a response, so we'd like to release them to go on someone else's list." Ask for more names, if you need them, or permission for your group to do its own recruiting. Likewise, once people show interest in being part of the group you lead, be sure to let the church staff know who you'll be taking care of.

Can You Identify the Ripest Fruit?

It makes sense to prioritize your contact work, whenever allowable, so that you can have the most fruit for the least amount of invitations. Of all the people you could invite, who are the most likely to respond? Some people are in a condition of needing relationships. Usually the newest members and visitors of your church are among the most hungry for new connections.

How to Invite #4: Prioritize the contact list.

Here are some possible priorities to consider:

1. New visitors.
2. Newest members.
3. Unchurched friends in the workplace and neighborhood.
4. Uninvolved members and adherents.
5. Referrals from surveys or from staff contacts.

Groups who invite generally find and hold more people than those who don't. Most first-time guests to a church service or small group will make a silent evaluation such as, "I think we'll like it here" or "I don't think we passed the test." When those who are already "in" notice newcomers, greet them warmly, introduce them to friends, the probability is very high that the guest will come back. If church people treat them in a ho-hum fashion, they are far less likely to return.

What would happen if every 10th person in your church were a small group leader, another tenth were an apprentice, and another tenth were an assistant in a group? That means 3 out of 10 were actively open to building a relationship with visitors, with hopes of inviting them into a group: "I've got a group of friends who meet on Thursdays. We'd love to have you come over and meet everyone." In a church with lots of well-connected inviters, a new person will sooner or later find a place to be cared for and loved.

As you revisit and reprioritize your invitation list, remember to allow the emergence of relationships. They're more teased out through time than assigned. Opportunities for acquaintance making lead to natural and spontaneous invitations of "Come over and spend some time with us."

Some People Are Downright Irrepressible

How to Invite #5: Be warm and enthusiastic.

On a plane trip once, I struck up a conversation with the young woman sitting next to me. An Asian, she had grown up in a Buddhist home. During her university years, she heard the gospel and became a member of a campus church.

When she said that she was a professing Christian, but did not currently attend any local church, I asked her why not. "You know how Christian congregations are," she replied. "It takes a great deal to break into them socially. At this time in my life,

I just don't have the energy to try."

In many churches there is an appalling lack of contagious love, especially toward newcomers and those who seem "different." I have met people who hung around their church for five or more years, and yet still didn't feel accepted. This chapter offers an answer to that problem. It focuses on the importance of attracting people to a group meeting where they can build relationships as they mature in Christ.

In contrast to the experience of the woman I met on the airline, I have the privilege of being part of a church. Sometimes various members of the congregation I attend will phone me at home, fax me at work, or find me at church. My response is to make time for them whenever possible. Why? Because when I've heard from them I feel better. Even if my day is too full to squeeze in a conversation or phone call with them, I do so anyway. I know that an important benefit will come from our lives touching each other: The interchange will enable me to handle the next hour better.

If you become known as that kind of person, then lots of people will respond positively to you. They will be drawn to the chemistry of who you are. As such, they will be the people most likely to welcome your ministry. You can't minister to folks when you're forever chasing them; people will open their lives to you in direct relationship to their willingness to come alongside you.

My point? If you're responsible for inviting others to your meeting, then it's very important that you learn how to be a pleasant person. If you invite folks and they don't come, then perhaps they're not looking forward to meeting with you.

Sometimes the resistance is as simple as needing a toothbrush to cure bad breath. Other times it's a matter of learning the courtesy of being on time, so people aren't annoyed by your perpetually late arrivals. Maybe you need to learn how to be excited about being with other people. Or perhaps you need to develop a genuine smile and the skill of initiating questions that show your sincere interest in the other person.

Unfortunately, not every person who names the name of Christ as Lord and Savior is an approachable or pleasant person. Grumps push people away. People who are negative or who refuse to deal with their personal insecurities or quirks generally don't have a magnetic effect on others.

However, if God's Spirit is inside you, then something about you can become attractive enough that people will respond to you and want to be around you. Every contact contains the potential for advancing ministry. Yes, leadership includes individual prayer time, waiting time, preparation time, and review time, but be careful not to miss spending significant time with people! It's hard to influence people if you're not with them. That's why greetings and informal contacts are so important.

Every contact contains the potential for advancing ministry.

A friend of mine, Alan Nelson, wrote a book called the *Five-Minute Minister*. He observed that the really significant things he had seen over his years as a pastor occurred in bursts of just a few minutes. A contact at the bank or a conversation after a breakfast meeting can make a huge difference in someone else's day.

The best ministry generally doesn't occur *during* a group's meetings so much as *between* the meetings. Every chance you have to touch people between meetings helps them become excited enough to want to come to the next meeting. You can give multiple touches in many simple ways: a phone call, a card in the mail, an intentional reference to the person's name, a "hello" with a big smile, a hug or touch on the arm, if appropriate. Touches like these keep people warm and looking forward to the next time they see you.

Effective lay ministers, like championship teams, touch a lot. What counts is showing some excitement: positive energy, a big smile, warm grasp, quick hug—those are the tools through which caring is conveyed. This kind of contact expresses a sense of worth to people. As soon as they feel like they're valued, then the next thing you know, they become open to receiving your ministry.

As you reach out, the Holy Spirit works behind the scenes to nudge people toward the love of God. If the caregiving Christian is an affirming, positive, cheerful, or energetic person, then newcomers will be drawn more deeply into the relationship. As you allow your personality to be developed, the Holy Spirit will find you an easy tool to use!

People feel safe with you because they can say, "When I see that person coming, I want to smile inside." That kind of trust and rapport leads to high-morale meetings.

People need to leave most encounters with you thinking, "I feel better." Remember a most important reason for developing pastoral care within groups and teams: A small group can hug you on a regular basis. If you're not in a small group, you've got to stand in line to be loved.

If you're not in a small group, you've got to stand in line to be loved.

"Christian People ...Somehow Help Me Feel Better"

I once heard the testimony of a woman who was a multi-millionaire. She had experienced a difficult episode in her life when one of her children was drastically sick. "Each time the Christians I knew came to my home, I felt better," she said. "I'd been managing a chronic sickness for several months, and I reflected one day on who I wished would visit me," she continued. She decided that the medical community had its limits as did her friends in the business community. "But those Christian people, the ones who offer to pray when they come, they somehow help me feel better," she decided.

Over time, she wound up following her Christian acquaintances into a church setting where she was able to hear the Gospel. Today, the Lord has transformed her life. As one evidence, she gives millions of dollars to Christian causes. She will tell you that her interest in the Gospel started because of a positive response to Christians who, with a small visit, touched her life and won a hearing for the Gospel.

What kind of a leader do you want to become? Will you be someone so magnetic that people jump at an invitation coming from you? Do you want to be someone who is a tool in the masterful direction of the Holy Spirit? Don't miss any opportunity to be used mightily as an instrument of God's invitation.

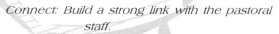

PREPARE

Connect: *Build a strong link with the pastoral staff.*

Recruit: *Keep your leadership nucleus fresh and growing.*

Invite: *Cultivate a larger contact group through enthusiasm and care.*

Prepare: Tailor a plan that you can prayerfully personalize to your group and apprentices.

Meet:

Bring:

Serve:

Win:

Seek:

CHAPTER 7

🔑 KEY FOUR:
PREPARE YOURSELF
TO LEAD THE MEETING

CHAPTER SUMMARY

❧

How to Prepare:
☑ 1. Make time for reflection and for seeking God's guidance.
☑ 2. Realize that each meeting starts and ends twice.
☑ 3. Review the group's need for loving, learning, tasking, and maintaining.
☑ 4. Design an agenda that you will personalize to your group.
☑ 5. Decide what leadership roles you'll ask others to take.

❧

"**D**EAR LORD, I NEED HELP," PRAYED JACK AS HE GUNNED his car through another yellow light. "I worked too late today and now this rush-hour traffic is terrible. I'll have only a half hour at home. I need to spend it eating dinner, or else I'll fade out halfway through tonight's meeting."

"I'm simply not prepared to lead the group tonight. I should have gone over the Bible passage and study questions yesterday. I should have made time to work with my apprentice or to give the Colemans a call like I promised. Jesus, won't you please show up tonight? If You don't, it's going to be a bomb."

More often than Jack liked to admit it, these desperation prayers were his primary way of getting himself ready for the weekly small group he led. In his heart he wanted to be a good leader, but procrastination often did him in. Then a heavy sense of guilt would dampen his spirit.

The meetings would usually be mediocre, leaving Jack both grateful and relieved. However, he was too embarrassed to admit he needed help, even to his apprentice. He feared that a confession of inadequacy would cause his apprentice (see Chapter 5) to become disillusioned.

The Most Important Preparation Step

Suppose Jack goes to his "coach" for advice. "I've blocked out Saturday afternoon to prepare for next week's meeting," he says. "I can think of 20 ways to spend that time—I could invite my apprentice over, I could phone various group members or our recent visitor, I could tape record some songs for us to sing, or I could call *you*! Where do I start?"

> *How to Prepare #1: Make time for reflection and for seeking God's guidance.*

In recent months, Jack's coach has sensed Jack's frustration over the meeting preparation and has been praying for an opportunity to talk about it. Here is the opportunity. What kinds of things need to be said?

The following sequence represents one possible approach.

The coach might affirm that it takes quality quiet time to get ready to lead a group meeting. If Jack hopes to be an instrument of the Lord in touching the lives of people, he needs to set aside a block of time, free from distractions. Then, when he has become quiet enough, he can be receptive if God wants to nudge him. In today's fast-paced, non-contemplative world, it usually requires diligent effort to stop long enough to ask, "Lord, is there anything You would like to put into the group's life at this coming meeting?"

It takes quality quiet time to get ready to lead a group meeting.

The coach might also help Jack on how to pray: "As you prayerfully ponder your upcoming group meeting, try not to think first about yourself and your own concerns. Rather, mentally review your group face by face, name by name, and pray for those people. Often, as you pray for others, the Holy Spirit will alert you to their specific needs."

"Ideas will often occur to you as you pray. Perhaps the Holy Spirit will impress someone's need on your heart with such conviction that you'll have to force yourself to sit quietly, rather than running to the phone to place a call. There will be times you ought to interrupt your planning time, go immediately to the phone, and talk with people."

Small groups are ideal settings for people to use their spiritual gifts as they put to practice the one-another commands of Scripture—loving one another (John 13:34, 35; 15:12, 17; Romans 13:8; 1 Thessalonians 4:9; 1 Peter 1:22; 4:8; 1 John 3:11, 23; 4:7, 11, 12; 2 John 5), encouraging one another (1 Thessalonians 4:18; 5:11; Hebrews 3:13; 10:25), bearing one another's burdens (Galatians 6:2), and even bringing one another back if we "should wander from the truth" (James 5:19). The Spirit of God becomes active in another person's life through Christian leaders like the coach, urging and prompting members to make the touches needed.

In short, whatever type of group a person leads, the leader must start the preparations with a quiet, reflective regard for the people in the group. Intercessory prayer will sensitize the leader to the needs of those people. In presenting Key Nine (page 173), this book will comment further on how to develop a lifestyle that regularly cultivates time for reflection and for seeking God's guidance. Thus when the first group participant arrives for the meeting, the group leader's head will be clear. Beginning with a personal touch and greeting, the leader can help open participants to receive whatever God has for them at that particular gathering.

Different Groups Run by Different Clocks

Some cultures are time-sensitive. Others are event-oriented. Americans tend to be clock oriented if they are of Northern European descent, if they've spent years in an educational community, or if they work for large corporations. Are you a person who carries a planning calendar broken into quarter-hour time segments or who measures activities in terms of minutes? If so, then starting on time is probably very important to you.

How to Prepare #2: Realize that each meeting starts and ends twice.

Or perhaps you're from a Southern European, African, or Latino culture. If so, you may be more event oriented. Getting there and being with people is far more important than the precise minute you begin. According to that outlook, things start when they start and end when they end.

As you anticipate the agenda for your meeting, you neither want to bend people out of shape nor frustrate their relational sensitivities. Where are you on the spectrum that places event orientation on one end and time orientation on the other? Where are the people in your group? In most cases, your meetings will meet with greatest satisfaction if you acknowledge an official starting and stopping time for the benefit of those with minute-sensitive orientations.

Then, barring emergencies, try to deliver on your promise.

Groups Have "Unofficial" and "Official" Starting Times

Remember that ministry begins as soon as the first participant arrives—or even as people meet each other to travel together to the meeting. The "pre-meeting" informal interaction time could be as short as two or three minutes, such as at a lunch-hour support group that gathers in the company cafeteria. Or it could cover 20 or more minutes in other contexts.

Thus one-another ministry can take place before you officially start, as well as after you officially stop. Important opportunities also exist for between-meeting ministry. In short, most groups provide a lot of avenues in which members can touch each other.

Next comes the more formal beginning. Very few groups can focus without a "get ready, get set, let's go" pattern. The "get ready" is the equivalent of a two-minute warning, the "get set" marks half a minute, and the "let's go" is the official start.

You can set up that pattern in the habits of your people. For example, a certain background song might signal a message of "all right, folks, when the song ends, we'll start." If there are children present or involved, their movement often becomes the cue: "Parents, we'll be starting shortly, so you might want to get your children settled." Some groups use a formal prayer to designate their start mark while others use a chorus that everyone sings.

The important factor is that someone takes the initiative to formally commence the meeting. If the leader has a tendency to be distracted in relationships, then perhaps the apprentice can be the one to introduce a meeting's visible starting cues.

There is no "right" way to begin a meeting. You'll need to experiment until you find a fresh and workable pattern for your group. It is usually wise, if your group involves time-sensitive people, to try to make it happen within 5 minutes of the announced start time. You will reward their punctuality and work within their comfort zone.

There is no "right" way to begin a meeting.

Getting Acquainted Is Important

Do not underestimate the importance of greetings, touches, and other get-acquainted activities. A warm smile, a sincere handshake, an affirming word, a brotherly hug—these brief encounters can set the tone for an entire meeting. They make a first impression of friendliness. They can help group members adopt an attitude of expectancy and trust. They can add courage to faith. They can strengthen someone's resolve to do serious business with God at the meeting.

Groups End Once, Twice, and Maybe Thrice

"The meeting went too long" should rarely be the reason first-time guests cite for why they don't come back a second time. Nor should it be a frequent reason people drop out of the group. If your meetings regularly go beyond 90 minutes, consider creating a window in which it is socially acceptable for people to leave:

• "Since our discussion has gone unusually long tonight, let's pause to have our snack time now."

• "For our prayer time, we'll break into smaller groups and maybe we'll designate John as the cluster leader for everyone who needs to pray more quickly and head home soon."

• "Our attendance today looks like it's at an all-time high, so we're running a bit slower than usual. Let's stand up, stretch, and if anyone needs to slip out at this point, we'll miss you, but we understand."

Even after the meeting reaches an official ending point for everyone, you will have people linger afterwards to talk with yourself or each other. Sometimes people walk out to their cars or the subway stop, and there resume the one-another ministry that was part of the official group time.

To end a meeting at about the time you intend it to stop, you need a sense of how much time you will spend on each part. Those variables will depend on the goal of your group, the life stage of the group, the personalities represented, and other factors, as presented in the rest of this chapter.

Some Groups Are More Like Mary, Others Like Martha

A lot of people will never be able to relate to the church or the gospel if you don't give them a chance to do so while swinging a hammer. Or planting flowers with you. Or doing some other kind of service project. Why? Because they're hands-first people like Martha (see Luke 10:38-42).

How to Prepare #3: Review the group's need for loving, learning, tasking, and maintaining.

Other people are the people-first sort like Mary. They're attracted to highly relational settings such as care groups or intimate Sunday school classes.

All the groups in your church can be roughly classified according to one of these two kinds. They either gather around sharing a common interest or doing a common task. Social psychologists, after years of study, have not been able to improve on these two very simple variations as to type and purpose.

Both Mary and Martha would find their place according to these two categories. Mary, who sat at Jesus' feet, would be in the interest group. Meanwhile Martha was fixing lunch. She would seek out a task group, such as the cooking crew.

A sense of community can exist in both types of groups, but both usually need help to achieve it. People who prefer action stuff, such as parking lot attendants or ushers, can come across as surly or grumpy when they focus more on parking correctly or guarding a door than on making people feel welcome in the house of God. As Jesus had to remind Martha, it's important to spend time communing with Jesus (Luke 10:38-42). Similarly, interest groups—Bible studies, 12-step recovery groups, prayer circles, and the like—can become very self preoccupied if you don't occasionally get them to do a task.

Why do choirs become places of criticism or infighting? Because the task of singing does not, in itself, ensure the spiritual development of the singer. You've got to stop occasionally, say prayers for one another, take each other's personal struggles into account, or you will not have a spiritual music program, no matter how excellent the quality is. A group that gathers around a common action will increasingly become fatigued without mutual support and encouragement.

Why do care groups sometimes seem cliquish? A group that meets around a common interest can become ingrown if it doesn't do something for someone else.

Both groups have a need for what the other has. The task group needs more loving amongst themselves; the interest group needs more serving of others.

Renewal occurs in both groups when you nudge them toward what's missing. Renewal for the shared-interest group comes through service; renewal for a task group occurs in community where members take time to love each other.

Similarly, either type of group can be intentional about showing the love of Christ to those who are outside the church or outside the faith.

In both types of groups, the group leader's role is to see to it that the participants receive the pastoring they need. All humans need love, support, and encouragement. Do they feel loved and cared for? As they do, the group will be healthier.

The work of the paid pastor, as a professional, is to see to it that those lay leaders get the resourcing they need in order to lead a group. What can a paid pastor do to increase the soul care in each of these kinds of groups? "Mary" groups must be challenged to work and to serve. "Martha" groups must be encouraged to come away for prayer and communion with God.

How ...to increase the soul care...? "Mary" groups must be challenged to work and to serve. "Martha" groups must be encouraged to come away for prayer and communion with God.

Your Group Has "Generic" Elements

Have you ever experienced a snow cone or an Italian Ice? Both start with shaved ice as the base ingredient. Then a coloring and taste agent are added to create a distinctive flavor.

Similarly, all church groups share something in common: the base ingredient of community. For them, the "shaved ice" is the Holy Spirit revealed in the pastoral care that occurs when people listen to each other and feel soothed and cared for. The small group leader facilitates community building. Each group's specific task, whether intercessory prayer, helping the homeless find jobs, or whatever, is like the snow cone syrups—whether raspberry, lemon, or grape.

Just as it's possible to discover the generic qualities associated with a snow cone, so also you can identify the generic ingredients associated with virtually every type of small group. Such a finding is often helpful to leaders because it can lead to new perspectives on how to shape your meeting agenda and prioritize your time usage.

Just as it's possible to discover the generic qualities associated with a snow cone, so also you can identify the generic ingredients associated with virtually every type of small group.

In the most general sense your group, regardless of its stated purpose, will do four things every time it meets.

• **Love.** Whether you call it care, encouragement, mutual support, listening and sharing, one-another ministry, nurture, or fellowship, every small group spends some amount of its meeting time with members building one another up and reaching out to each other.

• **Learning.** Similarly every small group does a bit of learning at each meeting. Virtually no church-related group meeting will conclude without some of the agenda, from a couple of minutes to virtually the entire time, being focused on studying, pondering, examining, reading, analyzing, or investigating some aspect of the Christian's beliefs or behaviors. Sometimes the content is verbal, such as when participants, listen to a "here's how we ushers can make guests feel welcome" instruction, or hear "missionary report" information as presented to an intercessory prayer group. Sometimes the group's learning text is a book, ranging from such classics as *Pilgrim's Progress* to recent releases by popular Christian authors. Most frequently the text is the Bible itself, perhaps supplemented by a study guide or reference notes.

• **Tasking.** To one degree or another, every group does something that benefits people outside the group. Parking-lot teams and choirs are almost entirely focused on task. Sunday school classes, support groups, and Bible studies may go as a group to serve non-members only occasionally, such as when they volunteer to handle crafts for vacation Bible school.

• **Maintaining.** Each regularly meeting small group will need to take a few minutes of its time together to address scheduling and equipment topics: "Will we meet during Thanksgiving week?" "Who's bringing the snack next week?" "In light of Carol's new baby, should we begin paying our sitter a little more?" and "Does someone have an extra portable crib that our sitter could use?"

Small groups can generally be matched to one of three generic types. Of the first three ingredients listed above, which one stimulates the most energy in *your* group? For example, in *care groups*, the larger part of time goes to "loving." In *Bible study groups*, the "learning" part will occupy the majority of the agenda. In *committees and ministry teams*, participants do most of their work "tasking" on behalf

91

of others.

These categories are helpful to maintaining balance in your group. In most cases task-oriented groups like ushers and handbell choirs will be healthier if they add more time for loving. Similarly most loving groups like care circles or fellowship groups will function better if they contain a degree of tasking.

It Is Important to Plan Well

The above-described categories of loving, learning, and tasking can also guide you in planning an appropriate agenda. As you prepare to face the group, at least two clusters of questions are helpful to ponder:

How to Prepare #4: Design an agenda that you will personalize to your group.

First, what will we do, in what order, how long will we spend on each, and how will we begin and end? Second, is there a message, burden, or Bible passage that ought to be discussed or delivered?

Whatever you do to begin and structure your meeting, if you have put together your meeting well, you can come to the meeting with your mind focused. By being freed from anxiety about what you intend to do, you can focus on the individuals present. Your sensitivity to people's needs will show itself in the game plan you follow and the roles you assign different participants.

You'll have a sense of anticipation because you've had each person specifically in mind during your preparation. You've prayed for each person. You'll have a Bible content ready. You're ready and eager for God to show up in the lives of those present. Your meeting's flow of events will perhaps contain many of the following:

- Arriving/mixing
- Opening
- Acknowledging God's goodness
- Learning and discussing
- Loving and listening
- Praying
- Announcing
- Closing
- Lingering and leaving

Always bear in mind that in a small group, the study of informational content or the accomplishing of a task is not nearly as important as the receiving of God's truth. It's not as important that you accomplish a task, such as preparing coffee for each Sunday's fellowship time, as that you build and model Christian community. You're not going to be teaching lessons as your primary objective, so much as caring for people. People don't care how skilled you are nearly as much as they want to know that you care about them. People don't care how much you know unless they know how much you care.

People don't care how much you know unless they know how much you care.

Worship in Small Groups, Mini-Churches, and House Churches

Most groups that hold regular meetings begin by acknowledging God's greatness and goodness. This activity can be short, such as the reading of a Psalm, or it can go longer, such as prayers in which many group members participate.

You might not want to label these moments as worship, however. It's important not to turn the small group or Sunday school class into a little congregation by duplicating what occurs in large-group settings. Small groups are a distinctive part of the larger experience of a church. You can worship in as large a meeting as you can assemble, but it's difficult to listen to one another in a large meeting. Certainly you need to acknowledge God's presence and worth, but reserve extended praise to the formal worship services of the church.

The uniqueness of a small-group setting is that it focuses on treating people as individuals. Thus you want to keep the amount of worship in balance with other activities under normal circumstances. In fact, one of the distinguishing marks of groups that label themselves as "house churches" or "mini-churches" is that they sometimes are more known as worshipping units of the church than as caring units. When the worship component dominates the agenda in a small group, it generally does so at a loss of one-another ministry. Groups that call themselves house churches or mini-churches also tend to restrict leadership to officially designated elders, halting expansion due to the inevitable crisis of not enough available leadership. One church I examined had a waiting list of six months to get invited to a mini-church, due to a shortage of elders.

Tips on Studying God's Word

Small groups offer an ideal social context for personalized Bible application. If your group's interaction with Scripture doesn't focus on the question of how the Bible will affect your life this week, then you're missing a great advantage that your group can provide.

Most small-group meetings will contain a message taken from the Bible. It will be short or long depending on the type of group. Sunday school classes or home Bible studies tend to allot much of their time to Scripture study. Task teams such as a trustee board may feature only a brief devotional thought taken from Scripture in the opening moments of their gatherings.

As you prepare, here's one way to study the Bible. This process can apply whether or not you are using curriculum and study guides.

1. **Pray.** As you commit your study time to God, invite the Holy Spirit to make the Word come alive in your heart.

Your job as group leader is to prepare first in prayer. Open your heart by asking: "What is the burden of the Lord for this particular upcoming meeting?" and "What does God want to see happen because Christians have been exposed to fellow believers and to Holy Scripture?"

2. **Reflect.** Read and meditate on the text. Write down the insights God seems to be teaching you. What does it teach you about God? God's principles? God's people? God's plan for the world?

In order for you to be adequately prepared for the Biblical materials part of your small group meeting, you want to exercise care as you review the text or texts. Studying the Bible is not a terribly complicated operation. If you listen during the normal teaching ministries of your church, perhaps even taking notes, then you're equipping yourself to handle any Bible-related questions that arise in the small-group meeting.

In the particular passage at hand, first read it several times. Perhaps use several different translations so as to avail yourself of the work of many Bible scholars. You may need to check with your church's leadership for a list of recommended translations.

3. **Expand.** Learn the larger context of your passage or book. Seek to understand what the passage meant to the original hearers or recipients.

As you explore related Bible passages, keep asking yourself, "How do these verses fit into the overall context of God's dealings with His people?" The longer you are a student of God's Word, the better you will become at addressing this question. Some of the most common Bible-application mistakes stem from not understanding how a particular passage fits into God's overall plan for those who follow Him. Bible dictionaries, concordances, and study Bibles will be helpful in pointing you to appropriate cross-references. They may also help you understand unusual customs, difficult expressions, relevant historical circumstances and the like.

Next it may be appropriate to read commentaries. Your pastor, denominational publishing house, or local Christian bookstore can suggest which of these tools would be most appropriate. Most commentaries highlight the findings of one or more Bible scholars who have studied the passage in depth and perhaps also gleaned from Christians in times past who have interpreted and applied the passage.

Through this "expand" process, review the insights you wrote down earlier. Are they consistent with what you are learning? Continue to add new notes about what God is teaching you.

4. **Apply.** Ask "so what?" questions. These will help you apply the passage to your life today. Examples include: "How does God want to change my life as a result of this teaching?" "What am I going to do about it?" "What can our group do about it?" "How can we be obedient, both individually and as part of the church?"

During your study process, you may gain impressions as to how this portion of Scripture applies to your own life. Sometimes the Spirit of God will convict you about your own attitudes and behaviors. If you bow in obedience to these divine promptings, you'll be modeling the kind of behaviors and attitudes that everyone in the group will need in order to be spiritually effective.

Here's one way to study the Bible...
1. *Pray* – Invite the Holy Spirit to make the
     Word come alive in your heart.
2. *Reflect* – Read and meditate on the text.
3. *Expand* – Learn the larger context of
     your passage or book.
4. *Apply* – Ask "so what?" questions.

After you have digested the passage and applied it personally, you are ready to think about how to present it in the group context. You can choose between a range of presentational formats, ranging from a brief classroom-style lecture to a highly participatory discussion. You can utilize any number of teaching aids, such as preprinted outlines, charts, or illustrative videos. Chances are that your church has a resource library or other opportunities for you to receive training in principles of effective learning.

Remember, however, that your presentation skills are not the chief way to measure your proficiency as a leader. A care group is not a class; it is a place of loving where truth is made real to current experience. At issue is not how good you sound, but how people are changed to be open to the work of the Spirit of God as you minister to them.

Indeed, whatever text the Spirit of God nudges you to follow, remember that the imparting of information is not nearly as important as the receiving and applying of it. You want group participants to take its truths to heart and wrestle with them, rather than to say, "Thanks but no thanks." The seriousness people bring to applying the Word to their lives stems from their feelings of being accepted by the group itself.

**The seriousness people bring to applying
the Word stems from their feelings of being
accepted by the group itself.**

What about Curriculum?

There is no lack of literature or resources on the topic of small groups. At latest count, more than 50 publishers offer a combined total of almost 2,000 small group books and other related materials for adults who participate in church-related groups. Your pastor, church Christian education director, coach, or fellow group leaders can point you to a range of options they feel are doctrinally appropriate. They may supply you with curriculum linked to the public preaching that occurs in your church. Or perhaps they'll hand you a catalog or book that describes many approved curriculum options available. You may be encouraged to make your own recommendation which they would then approve.

Who will decide what to teach? Some leaders self-select a topic or focus, based on the known needs and interests of group members. In other cases the group chooses the theme, such as a book of the Bible which the group studies one piece at a time. Sometimes church leaders assign the content, such as the text of the morning sermon. Liturgical churches might follow the Scripture passages presented in a lectionary.

If you do use a curriculum, the following qualities are especially important to help your group reach deeper levels of spiritual community. As you review curriculum, consider the kind of study guide that is:

• *Application-oriented.* Does it lead the group to a practical application of Scripture truths that can enable each person to mature in Christ?

• *Discussion-friendly.* Does it feature questions designed to help the group meaningfully dialog together?

• *Developmentally appropriate.* Does it use language and concepts that are readily understandable by the group? Is it suitable for the present life stage of your group?

• *Attention-retaining.* Does its approach to learning contain enough variety, creativity, and challenge for your group to retain maximum possible interest in learning?

• *Relevant.* Does the curriculum help the group focus on those needs within the group that the Holy Spirit seems to want to be addressed at this particular time in the life of the group?

To help your group reach deeper levels of spiritual community ...consider curriculum that is:
- *Application-oriented*
- *Discussion-friendly*
- *Developmentally appropriate*
- *Attention-retaining*
- *Relevant*

While many excellent curriculum options are available today, what is generally lacking is a unified theory to cope with all the variations out there. The values highlighted in *Nine Keys to Effective Small Group Leadership* do not ask you to give up your allegiance to a particular curriculum. Rather, they create a relational, supervisory, managerial, visionary approach to more effective group leadership. Their intent is to brighten the colors of virtually any curriculum system you use.

The Relational Side of Group Life

Don't underestimate the importance of building relationships through your group. Your group's time for members to become better acquainted with one another, unfolding their week for comment, can be as brief as a "summary sentence" by each person about the most interesting thing that happened since the last meeting. Or each person can be encouraged to provide great detail about their experiences and answered prayers since the last meeting.

Lyman Coleman and other trainers in small-group methodology have gathered compelling evidence that an ice-breaker experience at the beginning of the meeting inevitably deepens the Bible application and enriches the personal storytelling later on. Groups go through stages, similar to the stages in life, from forming (birth), through storming, norming, conforming, and performing (maturity). Many groups also experience a reforming stage (giving birth and reconfiguring). Crowd-breaker exercises are important at every point in a group's development, but especially so in the beginning weeks when the members are bonding with each other.

98

Groups go through stages ...forming, storming, norming, conforming ...performing ...and reforming.

What is the effect on group life when the church calendar calls for all groups to terminate at a certain time, such as at the end of Lent or at the beginning of the summer? The key is not to become curriculum focused. If your church's custom is to formalize the small-group year into seasons, there are still ways to remain group focused. Your pastoral staff may be quite open to a request from you that asks, "Can our group go beyond the regular season? Can we have potlucks, barbecues, and monthly gatherings as a way of staying in connection with each other?"

The vast majority of church pastoral staffs and boards do not mean to disempower their leaders in the "off" season. Calendar-driven approaches sometimes appear to disallow a group leader's ministry. If a group is not ready to break or suspend for the summer, there are usually legitimate ways of gaining permission to continue or to conduct reunions.

Give Thought to Your Announcements

At some point, often toward the beginning or ending of the meeting, you'll probably need a few minutes for announcements. This function plays an important role. We need to update ourselves on what's happening in the larger Body of Christ as represented by the entire congregation and by other Christian groups.

You and your group want to be effective members of the overall church team. The small group leader becomes an important information source for what's going on at church and in the larger Christian arena.

As you read your church's bulletin or newsletter, and as you acquaint yourself with other happenings that your people might join, you want to inspire and encourage a sense of excitement and anticipation for the kinds of things Christians are doing together, both at the local church level and across the globe. Be careful to balance those announcements so that you don't wind up being seen as disloyal to your local church because of your enthusiasm about events occurring elsewhere.

You create a hunger for participating in the larger Body of Christ by the personal attention you show. You develop that excitement as you prepare for your group meeting, looking for ways to share about other events in a way that seems natural to the flow of the meeting. In a small-group context, people place a lot of credence in things the leader says. In those churches marked by effective cell systems, the most persuasive place for announcements is not the bulletin or the pulpit but the small group. A pastor will reserve some of the church's most important announcements for the small groups, placing great importance and dependence on the church's group leaders to convey the kinds of concerns that are closest to the pastor's heart.

Sometimes You'll Need to Change Your Plan

When do you need to allow for variety in the pre-planned allotments of group time? There are two general situations.

First, the presence of a visitor is a worthy reason for a group to adjust its agenda. Newcomers need to be greeted, put at ease, and treated with a lavish amount of time. They need time to become acquainted with the rest of the group. They may slow things down, but not in a harmful way since they represent new life and energy.

Second, consider changing your plan when a member is in an overwhelmed condition. When a regular group member encounters trauma during the week, he or she will need more listening time, especially when family crises have occurred. At that point shrink your pre-planned tasks or learning time so you will have enough time to minister personally. When people feel cared for, they'll be back for many future meetings where over time they can gain all the learning they need or do lots of tasking.

Keep Strengthening the Leadership Nucleus

Many group participants find it wonderfully comforting to think that godly Christian leaders give time to think and pray about them, and to prepare a group meeting with a specific awareness of them in mind. A sense of anticipation often accompanies an expectation that "Our group leader has prepared the meeting in such a way that I can minister to others, and they can likewise minister to me."

The Christian faith was not designed as a Lone Ranger, "me and God alone" dynamic. Faith journeys involve community. Good groups are a highly mutual, one-another experience.

You need teamwork to develop an agenda, do the study work, facilitate the meeting, and coordinate the follow-up. Each of these dimensions of group leadership can be an important apprentice development time.

How to Prepare #5: Decide what leadership roles you'll ask others to take.

The setting of the agenda includes deciding the activities you will do personally, the responsibilities your apprentice will handle, and what you will ask others to do.

"Who's going to see to it that the refreshments will be cared for?" "What distractions should we anticipate?" "Who should we ask in advance to add a special touch through music, a poem, a praise report, or something else?"

You're thinking about not only the parts of the meeting, but who's going to do what part. One of your tasks is to do leadership development. You want to draw people out and let them shine in their area of motivation, interest, or expertise.

MEET

Connect: Build a strong link with the pastoral staff.

Recruit: Keep your leadership nucleus fresh and growing.

Invite: Cultivate a larger contact group through enthusiasm and care.

Prepare: Tailor a plan that you can prayerfully personalize to your group and apprentices.

 Meet: Convene your group in such a way that people genuinely experience the Body of Christ.

Bring:

Serve:

Win:

Seek:

CHAPTER 8

KEY FIVE:
MEET TOGETHER FOR
ONE-ANOTHER MINISTRY

CHAPTER SUMMARY

How to Meet:
☑ 1. Model an environment that facilitates mutual
      ministry.
☑ 2. Think through the anatomy of a typical small-
      group meeting.
☑ 3. Protect your group from the enemies of
      effectiveness.
☑ 4. Make regular adjustments designed to help
      newcomers feel welcome.
☑ 5. Remember that meetings have value in
      themselves because of spiritual gifts.

THE MOST TOUCHING STORY I'VE HEARD OF A GROUP AS A SAFE
place involved a young woman who had been abused, had gone
through two or three marriages, and had been forced to give up

custody of her children. She came to a small group led by friends of mine. As part of the welcome process, this couple asked her, "What would you hope for in your experience with this group?" She replied, "I'm hoping to find a safe place because I've been badly wounded. I need somewhere that will encourage me." The woman to her right, who herself was a relative newcomer to the group and not yet a believer, put her hand on the knee of this first-time guest. Then she said, "Honey, this is a safe place."

These small group leaders had achieved an important goal for any group, regardless of its stated purpose. An unbelieving seeker was able to say to a person who needed reassurance, "This is a group that is authentic and real, with people you can trust, potential friends who won't do you wrong."

Whatever kind of group you lead, your meetings need to be marked by times of joy, trust-building, and ministry one to another.

What Happens When Love Abounds

How to Meet #1: Model an environment that facilitates mutual ministry.

The most durable and life-changing dynamic in any kind of group occurs when members love each other. Even a between-services coffee committee won't be effective as a service team if they don't have relational time, pulling aside to concentrate on "heart" issues. Every group needs time for the care of human beings who have an eternal soul. In Bible terms, this action summarizes and fulfills God's law to love one another (see Romans 13:8-9, Galatians 5:14). Your group's morale will be determined not so much by how well they serve or by what they learn, but whether they think anybody loves them. One of the purposes of leadership in a church is to bring people together to learn to love each other.

> One of the purposes of leadership ...is to bring people together to learn to love each other.

The best way for people to learn that they're precious in God's sight is for someone, representing the Lord, to love and value them. Such concern communicates, "And you know, God loves you too." As 1 John asks, in effect, "If we've not loved our brother who we can see, how can we love God Who we can't see?" (see 1 John 4:20). God's unseen qualities become apparent and visible in human beings. Whatever kind of group you lead, if it's convened in Jesus' name, it needs to include some kind of care dimension where people know and experience the love of God.

First Corinthians 13, popularly known as the "love chapter," is one of the best places to find a description of Christ-like love. Here are the core verses:

(a)   Love is patient,
(b)   love is kind.
(c)   It does not envy,
(d)   it does not boast,
(e)   it is not proud.
(f)   It is not rude,
(g)   it is not self-seeking,
(h)   it is not easily angered,
(i)   it keeps no record of wrongs.
(j)   Love does not delight in evil
(k)   but rejoices with the truth.
(l)   It always protects,
(m)   always trusts,
(n)   always hopes,
(o)   always perseveres.
(p)   Love never fails.
(1 Corinthians 13:4-8)

What would happen if you compared the distinctive features of these verses with other injunctions for how Christians are to treat each other? I think you will see many parallels. For example, the first-listed quality above says that "love is patient." Elsewhere in the New Testament, believers are directed to *"Be patient*, bearing with one another in love" (Ephesians 4:2, emphasis added). A previous writing of mine, *Prepare Your Church for the Future*, highlights 59 "one another" commands of the New Testament in book-by-book order. Here's that same list clustered in alphabetical order. What additional parallels can you make with First Corinthians 13?

Accept one another ...as Christ accepted you (Romans 15:7)
Admonish one another (Colossians 3:16)
Bear with each other (Colossians 3:13)
Be at peace with one another (Mark 9:50)
Be devoted to one another in brotherly love (Romans 12:10)
Be kind and compassionate to one another (Ephesians 4:32)
Be patient, bearing with one another in love (Ephesians 4:2)
Build each other up (1 Thessalonians 5:11)
Carry each other's burdens (Galatians 6:2)
Clothe yourselves with humility toward one another (1 Peter 5:5)
Confess your sins to each other (James 5:16)
Consider others better than yourself (Philippians 2:3)
Do not grumble against each other (James 5:9)
Do not lie to each other (Colossians 3:9)
Do not slander one another (James 4:11)
Encourage each other (1 Thessalonians 4:18; 5:11; Hebrews 3:13; 10:25)
Forgive each other (Ephesians 4:32; Colossians 3:13)
Greet one another with a holy kiss (Romans 16:16; 1 Corinthians 16:20; 2 Corinthians 13:12; 1 Peter 5:14)
Have equal concern for each other (1 Corinthians 12:25)
Honor one another above yourselves (Romans 12:10)
Instruct one another (Romans 15:14)
Live in harmony with one another (Romans 12:16; 1 Peter 3:8)
Love one another (John 13:34, 34, 35; 15:12, 17; Romans 13:8; 1 Thessalonians 4:9; 1 Peter 1:22; 4:8; 1 John 3:11, 23; 4:7, 11, 12; 2 John 5)
Make your love increase and overflow for each other (1 Thessalonians 3:12)
Offer hospitality to one another without grumbling (1 Peter 4:9)
Pray for each other (James 5:16)
Serve one another in love (Galatians 5:13)
Spur one another on toward love and good deeds (Hebrews 10:24)

Speak to one another with psalms, hymns and spiritual songs (Ephesians 5:21)

[Stop] biting and devouring one another (Galatians 5:15)

Stop passing judgment on one another (Romans 14:13)

[Stop] provoking and envying each other (Galatians 5:26)

Submit to one another out of reverence for Christ (Ephesians 5:21)

Teach [one another] (Colossians 3:16)

Use whatever gift [you have] received to serve others (1 Peter 4:10)

Wash one another's feet (John 13:14)

Wait for each other ...when you come together to eat (1 Corinthians 11:33)

People today need a place where mutual one-another ministry is the key. By definition, then, such groups must not be consistently dominated by any one person, including the leader. If the only result is a me-to-you teaching or from-my-brain-to-yours transfer of content, then your gathering might not have enough "group" quality to be defined as a group! One-another ministry cannot occur without some form of discussion and interaction. The concept of mutual self care says that it's just as important what people say to each other as what the leader says.

Some Groups Use Covenants as "Ground Rules"

Covenants help establish ground rules in a group. It is not uncommon to find a membership contract that is as simple as a promise to attend for a certain number of weeks. Others elaborate numerous subjects such as attendance, participation, accountability, newcomer evangelism, availability outside meeting times, homework, individual study of passage or topic between meetings, prayer, openness, honesty, love, and/or confidentiality.

In some groups, the covenant is an oral agreement discussed in the opening session. Other groups write out and sign a covenant as a way of signifying a sacred promise that members make one to another.

Underneath most covenants is the idea of trust. In fact, the majority of group covenants are not enforceable, other than by asking an uncooperative person to leave the group. Thus mutual trust is vital to the success of any covenant. Here are three simple, trust-affirming covenants for your group to consider:

1. "Golden Rule" practice. In the Sermon on the Mount, Jesus says, "So in everything, do to others what you would have them do to you, for this sums up the Law and the Prophets" (Matthew 7:12). A simple promise for group members to make is to pledge, "I will not violate the Golden Rule in how I use information shared in the group." Confidentiality falls within the Golden Rule, as do several other of the above-listed topics.

2. "Edification" goal. The tone of any meeting is best if members agree *not* to discuss one another's faults—not the pastor's, not the group leader's, not their fellow group members', and not their spouse's. Such practices only tear down relationships. Instead, members could pledge, "I will restrict my confessions to my own sins and my own areas of needed improvement." Jesus' desire for His church, as Paul expresses in one passage about spiritual gifts, is "that the Body of Christ may be built up until we all reach unity in the faith and in the knowledge of the Son of God and become mature, attaining to the whole measure of the fullness of Christ ... Instead, speaking the truth in love, we will in all things grow up into him who is the Head, that is, Christ" (Ephesians 4:12-13, 15). Elsewhere Paul urges believers to "try to excel in gifts that build up the church" (1 Corinthians 14:12), gifts that lead to "strengthening, encouragement and comfort" (1 Corinthians 12:3).

3. Pursuit of truth framework. A third area of covenant affirms that the group will work to discover the mind of the Lord Jesus Christ. "I will ask, 'If Jesus were here, what would He do or think about this issue?'" Maturity in Christ involves walking and living as He would if He were physically present.

When these kinds of agreements are present, most of the other particulars are not needed. Shorter lists of expectations and simpler agreements make sense for most audiences. If your group prefers and really needs a more elaborate covenant statement, work with them to formulate one.

Three simple, trust-affirming covenants for your group to consider:
 1. "I will not violate the Golden Rule in how I use information shared in the group."
 2. "I will restrict my confessions to my own sins and my own areas of needed improvement."
 3. "I will ask, 'If Jesus were here, what would He do or think about this issue?'"

What Is the Anatomy of Your Group?

It's helpful for a leader to be aware of certain recognizable roles that often appear each time the group meets.

First there is the *leadership nucleus* (discussed in Chapter 5). It involves a *leader* and sometimes a co-leader, such as a spouse. It includes one or more *assistant leaders* who are serving in an apprentice role, training for the day when they will lead a group of their own. The leadership nucleus also includes one or two people filling a *host or hostess* function—opening their home, providing refreshments, and filling other necessary hospitality capacities.

How to Meet #2: Think through the anatomy of a typical small-group meeting.

In the likelihood that your group is taking responsibility for its own childcare arrangements, you may have a *designated childcare coordinator.* Intergenerational groups—ones that involve entire families—are growing in popularity. Even those groups sometimes take the children aside for a specialized activity.

Most groups will include *growing Christians* who are learning what their spiritual gifts are and are becoming deliberate in their use of those gifts. They are serious about going forward spiritually and they look to the group as a vital link in their growth.

People described as *seekers* are unhappy with something about their lives, and are looking for a safe place or a fuller relationship with God.

They've come to you or your group, thinking that you might have some of the answers they seek.

An *"extra-care-required" person* shows up in about one group out of two. This individual has needs and growth challenges that the group will be unable to accommodate. How will you be alerted when a participant has a level of neediness so great that it may destroy the group? Here are seven ways extra-care-required people might create turmoil. They regularly:

• Disagree with the leader: "No, you've got it all wrong" or "I was watching (name of program) on television, and he teaches differently."

• Attack someone else present, as in the case of a wife confessing the sins of her husband (or vice versa).

• Criticize the behaviors of others, such as making fun of group members.

• Dominate the discussion time by talking incessantly.

• Complain about the church services, staff or program.

• Behave rudely or cynically, such as saying, "That's a stupid, boneheaded statement."

• Refuse to cooperate with distraction control, through such actions as allowing their children to page them several times during each meeting.

Extra-care-required people might create turmoil. They regularly:

• **Disagree with the leader.**
• **Attack someone else present.**
• **Criticize the behaviors of others.**
• **Dominate the discussion time by talking incessantly.**
• **Complain about the church services, staff or program.**
• **Behave rudely or cynically.**
• **Refuse to cooperate with distraction control.**

How do you speak the truth in love to such people? Learning to deal with these situations in grace is the mark of a maturing leader. Here are several possible responses:

"This matter is important enough to you that I want to give it more focus than we can here in the meeting. Let's talk about this outside the meeting when we can have a one-on-one discussion." Honor the person, but deal firmly with him or else the rest of the group will not follow your leadership.

• "I want to honor your concern, but this is not the right forum. Will you see me afterwards?"

• "I don't want you out of my life, but I will not tolerate that behavior. If you choose to speak that way, you will not be allowed to participate in this group." Of course, this is best said privately.

Remember, as a Christian we don't have the same rights to free speech in God's kingdom that we may as a citizen in a free country. The Scripture doesn't give us the right to criticize in a group context; rather, we are to meet one-on-one with the person who has offended us.

The final person who might show up at your meeting is the *coach*, who occasionally drops by at your invitation or as prearranged. Hopefully your coach will be able to attend every few meetings. You want to be sure to introduce your coach as the person who helps you to prepare for and manage the ministry. Such positioning opens the door for help with certain problems that may arise. Your coach serves as a third party who can help you with difficult times or people.

For example, there are times in any group when a participant gets out of sorts with the leader. It is helpful to have an in-between person to bridge between the two parties. Or, if someone desperately needs to leave the group and join another, this is the opportunity for the coach to intervene. If the coach has previously met the person, you can say, "I think Brittany is struggling. Would you mind talking about whether this is the best group for her? I don't want to ask her because I don't want to communicate any feelings of rejection. Could you please give some guidance?"

The coach can then come up to Brittany and say, "Is this group working for you? I visit a number of different groups, and I couldn't help but notice that you were sitting quietly and seemed to be tense. Is

111

the chemistry okay?"

Brittany may then reply, "You're right, it's not working well but I don't have any courteous way of bowing out." Or she may say, "No, I have a burden that I'm not yet ready to share with the group, but I'm glad to be here."

Coaches can also help you with extra-care-required people, as described above and in chapter 5.

**It's helpful for a leader to be aware of certain recognizable roles that often appear each time the group meets:
...the leadership nucleus [leader, apprentice leader, and host or hostess]
...designated childcare coordinator
...growing Christians
...seekers
...extra-care-required persons
...visiting coach**

The more familiar you become with the anatomy of a group, the more you can develop the skills that enable you to facilitate mutual ministry. As a result, your group will become a more loving, caring, cell of interactive people who receive and administer support one to another. It will also become a place where an unbeliever can find safety while asking, "Is this the faith that I can embrace?"

Every Meeting Can Be a Positive Experience

How to Meet #3: Protect your group from the enemies of effectiveness.

It is important for your group meeting to be a positive experience for all present. For many in your group, their workplace is not a particularly affirming climate. For others, their home has been a source of abuse when they tried to share of themselves. For a handful, even church environments have been so full of shame and guilt that they approach group life scared and defensive about sharing on a "feelings" level. Any of these background circumstances

112

can cause a sense of reluctance as they enter a group.

As a result, it takes a special permission forum for people to feel safe enough to offer each other a portion of their personal biography. Here are several approaches you can use to facilitate an atmosphere of safety, genuine interest, and comfort in opening up on the feeling level. These skills will help you as a small group leader to successfully manage the complex mutual-ministry dynamics of a group:

• **Create a level playing field.** The opportunity to make a "childhood confession" seems to be a common thread that everyone can respond to except highly damaged people. Such questions center around each person's experiences as a child in a way that communicates "If you care to share, then we'd love to listen to you." The master at developing these "level playing field" perspectives is Lyman Coleman. His materials published by Serendipity House allow people to safely share at whatever level they're comfortable.

• **Use bonding questions.** One of the longest-used formulas asks: "What was the center of warmth in your home when you were growing up?" It's amazing what that question opens up. You'll be surprised by accounts of people raised in orphanages or people who struggled through their parents' divorce. All kinds of stuff comes out when people feel safe enough to disclose.

• **Avoid yes-no questions.** Questions that cannot be answered by a "yes" or "no" provoke the most ownership of response. For example, "What do you suppose Jesus would say about this?" is far more helpful than "Would Jesus have condoned this practice?"

• **Focus on discussion-sharing questions.** Learn to use wording that passes the discussion around in a group. Studies of personality type tell us that about half the population uses thinking as their preferred processing technique, while the other half uses more of a feeling approach. It's fair, then, to word application questions both along the lines of "what do you think?" and also "how do you feel?" Here are some helpful tools designed to facilitate such a discussion:

"Would you like to talk about that?" This question often shifts a statement of fact to a deeper-level of sharing.

"What do you think about that?" Offer time for others to comment.

"Who has seen this principle at work lately?" This question invites people to offer observations from their life and experience.
"Does anyone have a comment or additional point of view?" Instead of slamming someone who has a wrongheaded notion, you're helping them come to a more wise or more scriptural outlook.
"When would that idea be most helpful for others in this group?" This phrase helps people affirm or contradict others in a gracious way.

Focus on discussion-sharing questions...
"What do you think about that?"
"Who has seen this principle at work lately?"
"Does anyone have a comment or additional point of view?"
"When would that idea be most helpful for others of you in this group?"

• **Reposition statements that seem to stifle an ongoing search for truth.** It is possible to honor persons and acknowledge their opinions without agreeing with notions you think are wrongheaded. One approach is to reframe someone's statement by probing into the circumstances that led to it. Doing so positions people as opinion givers rather than authorities, framing their comments as expression of journey more than as absolute truth. It maintains someone's dignity while moving an assertion from "law" to one opinion among several. It often allows the group to process the idea without personal affront to the one who offered the comment.

Here are several comments that acknowledge the idea of process saying, in effect, "We assume your integrity; you're searching, you have a right to, you have a responsibility to, and we want to assist you in that quest."
"Do you think you'll feel the same way a few years from now?"
"I wonder how many others have come to the same conclusions as you have."

"You must have suffered a great deal of pain to express yourself as you do. Would you like to tell us a bit more of your story?"
"What experiences in your life have led you to feel as strongly as you do?"
"Your comment seems to come from a great deal of experience and thought." [Direct the next question to the group.] *"I wonder if others in the group have come to the same place in their understanding?"*

• **Ask permission to hold a discussion until later.** Sometimes you need to bring closure to a topic or tangent. Here are some transitional comments you could make that might place a heated exchange on hold while your group moves on to other emphases:
"That's something we can't do justice to in our limited time here tonight."
"That's something I'd love to explore with you when we have an opportunity."
"You seem to feel very strongly about that point of view. I'd be very interested after our meeting in hearing some of the experiences that led you to that conclusion."

• **Set an example by admitting the growth challenges you face.** You may need to learn some pride-swallowing phrases in how you communicate. To the group you may need to say on occasion:
"I don't know." Sometimes add, *"I'll have to find out"* or *"Who could help me find out?"*
"I was wrong." Sometimes add, *"You were right."*
Later in private with your coach, co-leader, or assistant leader you might find it helpful to ask:
"How do I handle this kind of situation?"
"Is there a more effective way to accomplish this?"
"What am I not seeing here?"

• **Offer non-threatening ways to pray.** Many discussion times conclude in prayer. Some people are comfortable, confident, and accustomed to praying long, intimate prayers. Others won't come again if they think you're going to force them to pray aloud.

Perhaps they're only to the point of preferring to follow a model prayer, such as the "Our Father who art in heaven" prayer that Jesus taught His disciples (see Matthew 6:5-15). Simple prayers can be followed by novices. Give them examples to follow and you'll embolden them to pray aloud.

Another option is to read a printed prayer. A third option is to pray and personalize the Scriptures themselves. For instance, if your group had read the verse, "Cast all your anxiety on him because he cares for you" (1 Peter 5:7), you might suggest that each participant follow this format in prayer: "Lord, I cast all my (name of care) upon you."

**Non-threatening ways to pray:
Follow a model prayer...
Read a printed prayer...
Pray and personalize the Scriptures...**

How to Avoid Hurt Feelings

Groups in which people are vulnerable inevitably contain situations that offend one or more of the group members. In many cases, character growth occurs best during these times of pain or awkwardness. You want to reduce the barriers that prevent the verbalizing of hurt, the giving and receiving of forgiveness, honesty about wounds, and a vulnerability about the kinds of behavior that cause us to keep our guard up.

In a small group I once led, we covered the verse that urges Christians to avoid "foolish talk or coarse joking" (Ephesians 5:4). At the conclusion, one fellow in the group replied, "Then what am I going to say? Most of our conversations at work center around insulting one another. We put a lot of work into finding clever ways to put each other down."

In response, we reminded each other that the purpose of most businesses is to make a living, which binds people into a context where they feel they must endure insults. A chief purpose of the church is to build people. My acquaintance decided to spend more energy treating people well, both at church and at work.

The purpose of most businesses is to make money, while a chief purpose of the church is to build people.

The higher the level of trust a group builds, the more significant the ministry that occurs. In the early church, Christians trusted their very lives to each other. Under times of persecution both then and now, a breach of confidence could mean someone else's death. For decades in the Soviet Union, China, and other countries, a betrayer who went to the authorities could prevent someone from finding employment or receiving higher education. Many people spent decades in prison because a neighbor or fellow small group member broke their trust.

The higher the level of trust a group builds, the more significant the ministry that occurs.

Through the way you lead the group, you can reduce the kind of behaviors that hinder the building up of each other:
• Foolish, belittling talk.
• Slamming or making fun of one another.
• Hurting each others' feelings.
• Teasing about each others' weaknesses.
• Harping on past failures or mistakes.
• Ignoring someone's serious request for help.

We can't be careless in speech or in failing to build one another up. We need to be treating one another with honor and dignity so that we can mutually bless one another. Most great achievements in the church and world can be traced to a situation where someone said, "You can do it" or "You can be a person who makes a difference in someone else's life." It's incredibly motivating to know that you can be a meaningful help to someone else.

Distractions Can Usually Be Controlled
Distractions are also enemies to effectiveness. Your group's meeting

117

space needs to be a guarded space. Most off-the-church-premises groups meet in multiple locations, and so you'll need to eliminate the distractions present at each site. Here are some preventative steps you or your apprentice can work with the host to think through as you deal with potential distractions:

• Pets—Hood the parrot, make sure the dog has been exercised, and cage the ferret.

• Airwaves—Cut off radio and television in the meeting room, arrange with the host home's teens to keep their stereos low, and make provision for the phone to be answered.

• Doorbells—Designate someone to welcome latecomers.

• Children—Develop an exit strategy for any children present who won't be able to participate in the entire meeting.

• Weather—Think through the implications on your meeting, if any, of rain storms, heat waves, or other changes in the weather.

Potential distractions:
- **Pets**
- **Airwaves**
- **Doorbells**
- **Children**
- **Weather**

Seating Arrangements Make a Big Difference

The forethought you put into room arrangements reveals whether or not you have a hospitality inclination. Some leaders don't look to the comfort needs of others, yet attention needs to go to the arrangement and cleanliness of the space, as well as to such issues as comfort, lighting, and distractions. That's the beauty of being part of a leadership nucleus: If you don't have sensitivities toward hospitality, then someone else probably does!

Second is an issue of communicative intent. If you set up the room in a classroom format, so only the leader can be seen by all, you've guaranteed a diminishment in the response of participants. If you set up the room so people have equal visual access with each other during

118

discussions, then they are far more likely to interact with the content on a personal level.

A Word about Legal Risks

Western society is prone to enter lawsuits quickly, often from frivolous or mean-spirited motives that in yesteryear could have been resolved by a personal letter or face-to-face confrontation. If you're going to host or invite a group onto your premises, a prudent path for reducing risks is to make sure you have homeowner's, renter's, or tenant's insurance that includes a standard legal defense clause. Also, in the way you lead the group, it is important to define your role not as a medical, legal, psychiatric, or clergy practitioner, but as a peer helper or people helper. The "helper" role is non-professional and it respects the existence and rights of the other formalized roles.

Certain mental health issues are outside your expertise or control; some of them may appear as the demonic, inclining you to think that they are purely spiritual matters. Even when that's the case, take great care to respect behaviors you don't understand. The novice doesn't know where the line is between where "fools rush in and where angels don't dare to tread." If you aren't sure how much caution to exercise in a given situation, ask your pastor or ministry supervisor.

When Your Group Is Open

All groups are open at some point to potential new members. Sometimes the open window occurs only during its first few weeks of existence. Other groups are open at different seasons, such as every couple of months when they do a service project or social function. A few groups open only rarely, such as when a member moves away and a replacement is needed.

How to Meet #4: Make regular adjustments designed to help newcomers feel welcome.

Even so-called closed groups are more open than they usually acknowledge. There is a simple explanation behind the mystery of how newcomers come into closed groups: Members classify friends differently than they do unknown strangers. Even closed groups welcome already-accepted "friends."

Many groups symbolize their desire to be outward focused by placing an open chair in their meetings and praying that God will use the group to fill the chair. The open chair is an evidence that the group is willing to receive new people without explanation or apology. It represents a permission that anyone in the group may bring a friend. More importantly, the open chair represents the commitment of the cell leadership to ask the Holy Spirit to help them find a receptive person to bring to the group.

Be careful not to confuse the open chair, as a symbol of openness, with the actual behaviors of openness. Open chairs in small groups may be both visible and invisible. However, Holy Spirit orchestrated results happen not just because an empty chair has been set out, but due to the cell leader's skill of relationship building or evangelistic recruitment beyond the group.

Evangelism ...happens not just because an empty chair has been set out, but due to the cell leader's skill of relationship building or evangelistic recruitment beyond the group.

This approach represents a major change from the model of assigning a teacher to a class. The kind of leaders who can make regular reports (Key One), recruit and train an apprentice (Key Two), and invite people to the group (Key Three) are also often able to relate to people who are not yet a part of a small-group meeting.

In the vast majority of cases, an openness to newcomers will provide many benefits to your group. As you facilitate the acquaintance of a newcomer with your group, you also help members get to know one another. The presence of newcomers gives everyone present a certain permission to share their story and their personal biographies.

Here are some questions you might use to begin a safe, bonding-quality discussion. Be selective, depending on what you know about your newcomer's level of spiritual commitment. "As we welcome Tran and Lee tonight, let's each introduce ourselves by sharing:

120

- ...what each of us likes best about our church."
- ...a time in our life where God significantly intervened."
- ...how we first heard about this group."
- ...where each of us was living at age 13."
- ...who was the first person in this group we met and under what circumstances."

This acquaintance-making time becomes a tone setter for the entire meeting, including the prayer time. As people voluntarily share, you will gain insights into their life. If they offer dilemmas to the group, either now or later in the meeting, they may be testing to see whether they can trust you with the true dilemma. People test you with superficial issues. If they feel treated well, they may disclose a more difficult challenge.

Model an Affirmer-Lover Mentality

How can you present truth in such a way that people such as visitors are able to receive it and not reject it? If people feel loved and affirmed, then their hearts become more open to hear and then embrace God's truth.

That's why the Bible urges us not just to communicate truth, but to be "speaking the truth in love," with the result that "we will in all things grow up into him who is the Head, that is, Christ" (Ephesians 4:15). Attitudes change when people feel that they are experiencing the love of God. Your responsibility is not to straighten out people so much as to use an encouraging approach that warms them to the work of God in their hearts. This supportive environment makes it easier for them to respond to the Holy Spirit's nudges and to surrender their misguided notions.

Jesus Himself had legions of angels that he could call against those who opposed Him. He had firepower available to him that no human army has possessed. Yet by choice He patiently showed the love of God, full of grace and truth. Visitors and members have a chance to see that same Jesus when they come into your group, if you are leading it effectively.

121

Be Alert to Life Outside the Group

How to Meet #5: Remember that meetings have value in themselves because of spiritual gifts.

Most literature about small groups, Sunday school classes, home Bible studies, and the like concerns itself with events during the 60- or 90-minute meeting. Yet what happens one-on-one *between* gatherings often contributes more to the effectiveness of your group than the actual gathering itself. If these outside-the-meeting dynamics, such as ministering to one another, are missing or just assumed, then the time together as a group will have only a hit-or-miss quality level.

What happens between gatherings one-on-one often contributes more to the effectiveness of your group than the actual meeting itself.

The key to effective ministry is found not so much in a cell group meeting as in empowered lay ministers. The meeting is the context that allows people to receive mutual care. Sometimes, though, the best care doesn't occur during the meeting.

What the meeting does is to give legitimacy to the care that happens between meetings. People who have the power to call the meeting also have a privilege, in the eyes of a group, that distinguishes them from most other church members. A mantle of permission continues to rest on anyone who is plugged into the church's authority structure, who has the blessing of the pastor, who will facilitate upcoming meetings, and who is available between meetings. These factors combine to give a special definition to the group leader as a spiritual helper of the members and potential members of your group.

What the meeting does is to give legitimacy to the care that happens between meetings.

Gift Usage Almost Can't Be Avoided

Your meeting, whatever its announced agenda or purpose, will probably do well simply because its membership has gathered together. Only when people interact with each other will they deepen their acquaintances, use their spiritual gifts, and develop a greater sense of unity as a result. An important value of a "meeting" is the face-to-face meeting.

A book I co-authored with Robert E. Logan, *Leading and Managing Your Church* (Revell, 1987), contains a chapter entitled "Using Spiritual Gifts to Focus Ministry." We pointed out that each Christian experiences a range of comfort when operating through spiritual gifts. That's where we're most effective. The teacher does best at teaching and the servant shines at serving.

However, what if the teacher is uncomfortable with what evangelists do? Suppose the teacher says so in a way that causes evangelists to stop using their gift? Or, what if the servant has problems with exhorters' approach to ministry, expresses the discomfort aloud, and pressures the exhorters into not exercising their gifts? In short, a church's or group's overall effectiveness expands or contracts on the basis of gift usage. Broad, multi-pronged ministry occurs in relation to whether Christians allow other believers to use gifts that they themselves do not possess.

A ...group's overall effectiveness expands or contracts ...in relation to whether Christians allow other believers to use gifts that they themselves do not possess.

Gift-based ministry is what God had in mind all along when He created the church (see Romans 12 and 1 Corinthians 12 to 14). Focus your efforts according to your own gifts. Allow others in your group to complement you by using the gifts God gave them. If you do so, your group will have a zone of potential ministry as large as the whole group's gifts combined. All will follow the faith of each gifted person and be built up by seeing the effect. (See Appendix C for a partial list of gift-identification and gift-mobilization instruments).

As a result of people coming together in the group you lead, will they love God more and appreciate what God has done in giving us a place in the body of Jesus Christ? Whenever the body of Jesus Christ gathers, especially in its small-group manifestation, there's an opportunity for Christians to show love one to another in the name of Jesus Christ. Your group is a vital part of what God is doing on Earth at this time in human history.

BRING

Connect: *Build a strong link with the pastoral staff.*

Recruit: *Keep your leadership nucleus fresh and growing.*

Invite: *Cultivate a larger contact group through enthusiasm and care.*

Prepare: *Tailor a plan that you can prayerfully personalize to your group and apprentices.*

Meet: *Convene your group in such a way that people genuinely experience the Body of Christ.*

Bring: Help each group member appreciate the whole church through larger corporate worship.

Serve:

Win:

Seek:

CHAPTER

9

🗝️ KEY SIX:
BRING YOUR GROUP TO WORSHIP

CHAPTER SUMMARY

How to Bring Your Group to Worship:
☑ 1. Protect the cell meeting as a listening place that
        emphasizes care.
☑ 2. Underscore the advantages of being part of a
        larger body.
☑ 3. Set an example by sitting with members of your
        group during worship.
☑ 4. Plan group events that overlap with worship
        services.
☑ 5. Work with your apprentice to lead group
        members into new service times.

A CCORDING TO GENESIS 24, ABRAHAM SENDS HIS CHIEF SER-
vant to find one of his relatives as a wife for his son Isaac.
Traveling to the area of Abraham's extended family, the servant

127

approaches a well and offers this prayer, "May it be that when I say to a girl, 'Please let down your jar that I may have a drink,' and she says, 'Drink, and I'll water your camels too'—let her be the one you have chosen for your servant Isaac" (verse 14). Before he finishes praying, a young lady offers to water all his camels. He asks her whose daughter she is and learns that she is a niece to Abraham. She is beautiful, unmarried, and very hospitable to the servant.

In response to this amazing series of events, the servant "bowed down and worshiped the Lord" (verse 26). He gets down on his face in gratitude to God. I can imagine him praying, "Sovereign Lord, here I travel all these miles and the first person I meet is a candidate, and perhaps the very person I'm looking for. This is an answer to my master's prayers and my own."

That kind of experience is where worship starts: a sense of being overwhelmed with God's goodness. A sense of gratitude wells up that erupts in attributing God's worth for who He is and what He's done. In today's vernacular, we say "Our God is an awesome God" or "God is good all the time!" Worship honors God and His work.

How to Bring #1: Protect the cell meeting as a listening place that emphasizes care.

The Best Settings for Worship

You can worship all alone, in a small group, or in a large coming together of the congregation before God. Worship is indeed a vital part of the Christian life (see 1 Chronicles 16:8-29, Psalm 100:4, Psalm 146:1-2, Mark 12:30, Galatians 4:6, Hebrews 13:15, 1 Peter 2:5-9, Revelation 4:8).

As a small-group leader, you want to teach people to turn their thoughts to God's goodness and greatness. By example and training, they need to grow deeper in their love for Him with all their heart, mind, soul, and strength (Matthew 22:37).

However, if you spend a lot of time worshiping in your small group, you won't do what the group is primarily focused on doing. Big meetings are wonderful for corporate worship, but not for being listened to. Small groups are ideal for sharing and caring. You need both settings to experience full Christian living.

Big meetings are wonderful for corporate worship, but not for being listened to.

As small groups grow beyond about 10 people, they tend to spend more and more time worshiping. The group leaders become excited: "Worship is really doing something for us because now we've got 20 and now almost 25."

That's usually a misdiagnosis, however. Once attendance passes 10 or 15, you aren't able to listen to them. In actuality many people are so frustrated at not being individually listened to that if you don't use the time for worship, they won't feel that it's worth their time coming.

Expanded worship in a small group is often a symptom of neglectfulness in caring. If you go beyond 5 or 10 minutes of worship in your small group meetings, you'll begin to take time away from the things that can happen only in a small-group context. Group members can worship alone or in a celebration-size gathering, but they can't find intimacy, accountability, opportunities for sharing, and other forms of one-another ministry outside the cell-size meeting.

Expanded worship in a small group is often a symptom of neglectfulness in caring.

The Need Not to Burn Out the Leader

As Key Four pointed out, small groups are not house churches. There is a distinction between a home-based small group and an intentional house-based church or mini-church. If the gathering is *not* part of a larger body, then it needs to worship. The most common range for house churches is 25 to 40 people—often with small groups that meet on the side at other times. Also house churches are usually limited in their leadership to those who occupy the equivalent of the role of elder.

In summary, it is vital that you maintain a connection and balance between the functions of cell groups and the larger-group worship services. Of those groups that grow to 17, 25, or 35 people, they almost always do so because of worship music—or they must have worship music because they grew. When you get past a dozen or so, since only a handful can share each week, you begin to reason that it makes more sense to formalize the teaching and do more music.

You thus grow yourself into a house church. The problem is that a volunteer group leader cannot do one-on-one ministry to everyone in a group that size without burning out, so it's not a reasonably sized unit for sharing. When it becomes a house church, the care needs of people are not going to be attended to without the threat of burning out the leadership. Protect the cell as a listening place for giving individual care to people.

Protect the cell as a listening place for giving individual care to people.

The Rhythm Between Cell and Celebration

Another reason not to do too much worship in the cell is so that people will have an added incentive to come to corporate worship. You want them to see the larger body. It's highly unlikely that your small group meeting in an office or home setting can sense the impact of a full choir singing an Easter cantata. You want them to experience other ministries—drama, choirs, musical ensembles, baptisms, and reports on mission trips. You realize the work of God is much broader than your cell. It's part of a larger

How to Bring #2: Underscore the advantages of being part of a larger body.

system. It is also good for your people to be exposed to more worship styles than are typically found in a small group, whether the exuberance of a victory march or the quietness of a chapel.

The various parts of the worship experience can also take them far beyond where they are spiritually, leading to small group discussions about Communion, baptismal rituals, blessings, and other things that are often part of being gathered together as a larger church. They will also spot opportunities for service, both as an individual and as part of a group, as they see other Christians using their talents as a way of worshiping God. Finally, through corporate worship your group will see the Christianity you're talking about being embraced by dozens or hundreds of other people. Such exposure does something for them, encouraging their hearts and giving added credibility to their faith.

Your group will see itself as part of a much larger system that has all kinds of resources available to it. It broadens their view of the Christian life. You have the opportunity to take them to meet other people that they wouldn't meet in the small group. Perhaps you'll introduce them to the church staff, recreational director, youth department, Christian education program, or counseling referral system. The more your people see the kinds of resources available to you, the more they will trust your ministry as a small group leader. It is important for your group to know that there are people training you and providing backup, and that you know how to find help for your group.

Sooner or later, you'll have someone in your group whose problems are so big that you can't manage them through their present crisis. Then you'll be able to say, "Remember Herman or Sally who we met at church? Did you know that he or she does referrals? Why don't we make an appointment to ask who you might see for further help on this matter?" You'll thus tie your people into this larger set of resources.

By bringing your group to worship, you're also helping the church staff trust you more. They build you up as a cell leader and you build them up as the staff. The partnership works both ways.

The best-fed Christians are ones who alternate between the splendor of the large meeting and the process of being listened to in the small meeting.

There's a divine rhythm between small group and large group. Cells, where loving occurs, create a pressure for worship service attendance. Cells have hugs and tears, but not much electricity ("dancing down the aisles"). The excitement of celebration will wear you out if you don't have a place to go to rest and talk it over, and that's what the cell is all about. The best-fed Christians are ones who alternate between the splendor of the large meeting and the process of being listened to in the small meeting.

Trends for the Future

Who is looking out for the attendance growth at your church's services of divine worship? In farming communities, it used to be Dad and Mom. What's happening increasingly is that if you as a small group leader don't focus on helping your people get to corporate worship, they won't value it. They won't realize the benefits of it. They need to be encouraged and trained to enter the service as participants, not just spectators.

If you as a small group leader don't focus on helping your people get to corporate worship, they won't value it.

Why? The Baby Buster generation (those born after 1964), and to a degree their predecessors the Baby Boomers (those born 1946-1964) have become secularized and have so little in common with the programs of the church as we have known "church" in times past. Thus the relationships established in the cell may be the only reason they have for wanting to make an entry into the wider church. When that time comes, if your church has side doors in place, the shift will occur. I predict that over the next decade or two, the shift in North America will move from churches whose "front door" (worship services) is the primary entry point to those churches that have "side doors" ready (small groups).

The church of the future looks like a place where we worship God in large groups, we nurture each other and do our service in small groups, and where those who give spiritual oversight are placing their highest leadership priority on forming leaders and giving them permission to minister.

The church of the future looks like a place where we worship God in large groups, we nurture each other and do our service in small groups, and where those who give spiritual oversight are placing their highest leadership priority on forming leaders and giving them permission to minister.

132

Don't Be Surprised If You Sit Together

As the relationships in your group strengthen over time, you may find yourselves accompanying each other into worship, so as to share the hour together. If group members don't want to sit near you, you need to find out why! Stated positively, it's a good sign when you can sit down and four or five group members are within touching range for you.

How to Bring #3: Set an example by sitting with members of your group during worship.

Set an expectation as you work with your group that you want them to come and worship *with* you; lead them to the service you'll be attending. However, don't try to force a retrofit. The most leadable people are the ones who have not yet developed a habit of attendance at a particular service of worship. Particularly if they're new converts, they won't have worship-time expectations set in concrete.

Cells Lay the Foundation for Multiple Services

Being at worship with your people also bears potential for growing the entire church. Healthy cells can enable a church to go to two, three, four, and even more services without wearing out the staff, either those volunteering time or those being paid! God doesn't excuse us from evangelism because our church building is full or almost full. In virtually every city and town, there's a large harvest out there. Just maybe the Lord wants more churches to reach more lost people by using their building a few more times each week.

There are four pieces that need to fit together in launching an additional service. Each of these parts can be based on a strategy of leadership development through small groups.

• First, a new service requires platform people needed for the various celebration arts. Most services need a speaking team, a technical team, a setup crew, and one or more groups of musicians. In most cases you can't use the same choir or lighting crew (or whatever) from other services because over time they'll burn out. The exception is if you rotate weekends: Drama Group A does all services on the first weekend of each month, Handbell Ensemble B will do all services on the second

133

weekend of each month, etc.

• Second, you need teams to handle crowd-control: ushers, greeters, parking lot guards, or whatever.

• Third, there's a Christian education dimension: either children's church or Christian education. This will probably involve teams of Sunday school workers, nursery workers, and the like.

• Finally, you need people—the congregation who will "come" to the service. Suppose your worship area seats 120. Why not use the team concept here as well? If the leadership nucleus in a dozen small groups will each take responsibility to birth and bring a new group, then voilà! The worship space will be full for that service.

Granted, existing groups with already established worship patterns generally are not eager to shift en masse to a new service time. However, newly organized groups filled with seekers and new Christians are often quite amenable to coming to a new worship service hour, such as earlier Sunday morning, Saturday evening, or whatever new slot you're opening up. If your group is instrumental in leading people to faith in Christ, it can be a very natural process for them to follow you as their leader to worship. The administrative support task is to provide the auxiliary childcare, children's Sunday school, youth classes, and so forth that those who attend the new service will require.

In Tokyo, Japan, I've heard you can't buy a new car until you demonstrate that you have a place to park it. The police station must know you have a specific, available parking spot before they will authorize you to obtain a new car. Having a new group that doesn't have room to attend corporate worship could pose a similar problem, but as with the Tokyo car buyer, you can reserve a space for them as the new service is being launched!

Of course there are exceptions caused by people's schedules and family needs. However, in general this "cell-driven" approach to building new worship services is one of the smoothest and most natural harvest strategies that assimilates new converts both into a small group and into the larger body of the church.

• First, as you connect with church leadership (Key One), you'll catch their vision—or gain permission—to reach the additional people that God may want to bring you.

• Second, as you learn how to reproduce yourself (Key Two), you'll make available the additional leadership needed to reach out into your church constituency and community.

• Third, as people start new groups (Key Three) and win people to Christ (Keys Seven and Eight), there will be an added need for new services as well as a willingness by these newcomers to be part of the new services.

How do you build worship services for a long-term future? Group by group. What kind of leaders are needed to produce this kind of service? Ones with a physical following, who can take people with them. If you're enough of a leader for them to come to a home and meet with you, then there's probably little difficulty in inviting them to worship together.

Seen this way, people at worship are part of a conglomerate plan. They are not there as individuals, nor are they an indistinguishable mass; rather they are a convention of small groups.

Group Life Invites a Larger Social Impact

When you as a leader invite your people to join the service you attend, and as you involve newcomers in your group, consider another step that will make it easier for newcomers to cross the bridge into church services. Arrange events before and after the worship service so there's an even larger social impact. Begin to structure the social outings

How to Bring #4: Plan group events that overlap with worship services.

and service projects of the group around a question like this: "Why don't we go out together after the service?"

I've known groups that regularly eat together before or after the worship service they attend together. Another goes from the worship service to assist in a soup kitchen. Another likes to go hiking together. Yet another takes turns going to various members' homes and doing home-repair projects as a group.

Do Leaders Have the Most Clout?

As described above, churches are discovering that they have an enormous power through their lay leaders to use their facilities in a more effective stewardship of their wealth. Most churches could make much better use of their worship areas if they had a way of arranging for participation in the various services they offer.

How to Bring #5: Work with your apprentice to lead group members into new service times.

It's just a matter of time before new seekers will find their way to your cell, and will go with you to a Saturday night, early Sunday morning, or some other alternate-hour service. As you become an effective leader and inviter into small group, in a matter of months or a year you will take them to the service hour that fits into the overall strategy of using your church's worship space and parking resources most effectively.

Be Part of Something Larger

People are looking for something to change their lives. They want contact with the Almighty. They want to know God is real. Musicians and dramatists are that special group of people who have the way of rallying our emotions and senses more effectively than almost any other class of people in a congregation. Animated pulpit preaching and teaching from God's Word has made a profound impact in every generation of the church's history.

Your small group is one part of a larger whole. Clergy in virtually any sized church would be thrilled to have a leader like you who moves others into worship with God's people and helps prepare the hearts that are becoming ready to receive the Savior.

SERVE

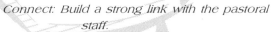

Connect: Build a strong link with the pastoral staff.

Recruit: Keep your leadership nucleus fresh and growing.

Invite: Cultivate a larger contact group through enthusiasm and care.

Prepare: Tailor a plan that you can prayerfully personalize to your group and apprentices.

Meet: Convene your group in such a way that people genuinely experience the Body of Christ.

Bring: Help each group member appreciate the whole church through larger corporate worship.

Serve: Make time to serve needs in and beyond the group.

Win:

Seek:

CHAPTER

10

🗝 KEY SEVEN:
SERVE THE GROUP
AND OTHERS BEYOND

CHAPTER SUMMARY

How to Serve Others:
☑ 1. Remember that serving is an important act in obeying God.
☑ 2. Continue in present serving capacities, realizing that you share important ministry with your pastor.
☑ 3. Listen carefully for personal needs disclosed in your group which you can meet.
☑ 4. Begin to extend acts of serving to people beyond your group.
☑ 5. Combine spiritual gifts and serving to build bridges and win a hearing for Christ.

A FRIEND OF MINE WHO LEADS A SMALL GROUP TOLD ME A story about one of their members, a single parent, who was facing the trauma of navigating her family through Christmas. In

139

that group also were a number of breadwinners, but at the time several of them were between jobs, facing hard times as a result.

These families got together, apart from the woman, and said, "She'll have a terrible time this Christmas because she has no savings, her husband has reneged on support, and her job pays poorly." They took up a collection that amounted to $400 cash and they handed it to her as she left the meeting.

A half hour later the group leader happened to glance out his window. He noticed that her car was still parked out at the curb. He went out to see if everything was okay.

She had been so moved by what had happened that she was still crying. She was sitting behind the wheel of her car, too teary-eyed to drive. Her spirit was touched by how deeply the group cared for her, placing a gift in her hands when they themselves had great needs.

Her children's Christmas that year was perhaps their best ever. More permanently, her whole perspective and demeanor changed as she learned what it means to experience God's love by being part of Christ's physical body on earth.

The Heart of the Gospel

In the first generation of the Christian era, Jesus' followers behaved likewise. They sold houses, farms, and possessions because they wanted to give to fellow believers who were undergoing persecution (see Acts 4:34-37).

How to Serve #1: Remember that serving is an important act in obeying God.

In Jesus' final teaching to the disciples before His crucifixion, He served their needs, in this case washing their dusty feet. Then he said, "By this all men will know that you are my disciples, if you love one another" (John 13:35). When we serve one another in Jesus' name, the world sees clearly that what we have is for real. Not only that, but when we give sacrificially, we grow personally.

When you help people, you invest in the only permanent entity under heaven. Nothing else will last for eternity. Christmas trees, Christmas gifts, and envelopes containing cash will disappear. The only way we can turn temporal wealth into something of durable contribution is by lavishing it on people. As one Christian has said, "I can't take it with me, so I'll send it ahead by giving it away."

As one Christian has said, "I can't take it with me, so I'll send it ahead by giving it away."

Didn't our Lord indeed give everything, including his life, for us? As He explained to His disciples, "Whoever wants to become great among you must be your servant, and whoever wants to be first must be slave of all. For even the Son of Man did not come to be served, but to serve, and to give his life as a ransom for many" (Mark 10:43-45).

Didn't Jesus also make constant sacrifices along the way? He deprived himself of a home—"the Son of Man has no place to lay his head" (Matthew 8:20). He deprived himself of sleep—He rose up "very early in the morning" (Mark 1:35). He placed Himself under the disciplines of the spiritual life, willingly giving of Himself for the benefit of others (see Philippians 2:5-11). And He called us to live likewise: "If anyone would come after me, he must deny himself and take up his cross daily and follow me" (Luke 9:23).

According to Scripture, service is a God-blessed thing to do. The writer of Proverbs said: "Whoever gives to the poor lends to the Lord" (Proverbs 19:17). That's a powerful statement! To be like Jesus, to follow His model, means to give of ourselves.

Therefore, in the context of your small group, it is wise to give love, time, energy, and sometimes even money to others. (Incidentally, don't encourage the *lending* of money between members of the group. Giving money is fine, but lending is a trap. Debt repayment issues inevitably cause problems. Also don't encourage the formation of personal businesses and investments between members of the group. The unforeseen consequences are usually enormous. Almost always, misunderstandings arise around the investing or lending of money. Griefs arise, relationships sour, and confidence is lost. Leave that kind of activity to an area disciplined by law).

141

Serving validates the life-transforming character of the gospel.

You as the leader will want to show people how to give and receive acts of charity in the context of the group. As Jesus taught His disciples when He washed their feet in the upper room, the Christian world is upside-down, where greatness is measured in humility. Serving validates the life-transforming character of the gospel.

Serving Handfuls, Not Masses

Greeting cards and cross-stitch murals sometimes contain the following expression: "God could not be everywhere so He made mothers." Biblically speaking, God *is* everywhere, but it is also true that He has used mothers (and fathers) as the threads that hold the fabric of a society together.

How to Serve #2: Continue in present serving capacities, realizing that you share important ministry with your pastor.

For years in North America, pastors have had the able assistance of mothers to keep the church going. Especially during our pre-Industrial eras, mothers took care of looking out for the upbringing of people. Lately, someone has been tampering with motherhood and fatherhood. Families just aren't what they used to be. There isn't enough nurturing to go around.

Most Christians today don't have the capacity to follow God with all their heart unless they have help along the way at critical choice points. It helps to have friends who are willing to ask, "Are you sure you want to do that?" "What would the Lord Jesus do if He were in your situation?" and other similar questions. It's in the absence of these rubber-meets-the-road encounters that we're in deep trouble as a society.

Caring relationships are the key to developing a church that gets down to where people live. Such a level of church health is not dependent on the energy of the pastor to visit, know, and personally be available to each member of the congregation. Rather, the critical factor surrounds the willingness of the pastor to make a partner out of a lay leader who will look after five to ten people, praying and serving them to safety.

This idea sounds simple, but it has enormous consequences. The typical North American pastor tries to serve the needs of about 100 people. Most clergy run out of strength, however, far sooner than they run out of people open to being touched in Jesus name.

I spoke with one pastor who ministered in a particularly underchurched area. "Have you considered another worship service?" I asked.

"Another service?" he said, almost with a look of fear.

"Sure," I continued. "Your facilities and existing schedule could handle it. What makes you hesitant?"

"Because they'd come!" he replied. "Our staff and lay leaders are too overloaded now. If I added twice the number of needs, it would burn them out."

There's something wrong with the attitude behind that reply. The issue is not church size; I've seen that attitude in flocks of 50, 500, and 5,000. At issue is the equation that says "more people" equals "more burden." If God's foundation of care is to stem from the pastor himself, then this pastor was right.

However, just before Jesus ascended to heaven, He set forth a better idea. He said, "...It is for your good that I am going away. Unless I go away, the Counselor will not come to you; but if I go, I will send him to you" (John 16:7, NIV). In essence, the Holy Spirit came so that Jesus could be everywhere. Jesus said, in effect, "All you have to do is get two or three Christians together, and I'll show up there in the midst of you." Jesus the Great Shepherd, unlike His human undershepherds, can be in millions of places at once. His mathematics say "more people" equals the potential for "more love, more equipping, more evangelism, and more discipleship." What a difference!

That strategy comes from the Master Himself! The Body of Christ is a wonderful phenomenon that has changed the role of the undershepherd from Pentecost until the end of the age. God's plan for taking care of people today is not the old lone-shepherd model in which "real ministry" requires the presence of an ordained minister.

Too many Christians live, perhaps without realizing it, back in Moses' day, when the best people could do was to yearn for the day when the Holy Spirit would visit everyone, not just the leaders. In one instance the Spirit rested on 70 of the elders and they began prophesying. Moses' assistant ran to Moses, asking that they be stopped. Moses replied, however, "...I only wish that all of the Lord's people were prophets, and that the Lord would put his Spirit upon them all!" (Numbers 11:29, TLB).

Back then, common wisdom was that a leader couldn't trust sharing the ministry with others. Yet God did put his Spirit on all people and we're still behaving like He hasn't. As the Apostle Peter explained in his Pentecost sermon, citing the prophecies of Joel, "'In the last days,' God says, 'I will pour out my Spirit on all people. Your sons and daughters will prophesy, your young men will see visions, your old men will dream dreams. Even on my servants, both men and women, I will pour out my Spirit in those days, and they will prophesy'" (Acts 2:17-18, NIV).

In virtually every case I have studied, churches lose more people to neglect than to schism.

Too many people see their pastor like a Moses figure—the only one who can do what needs to be done. Allowing the saints to become involved in the ministry creates all kind of wonderful consequences. Yes, sometimes people disobey God or abuse the privilege of the indwelling Holy Spirit, leading to schism, prideful independence, and a damaged testimony before the world.

Sometimes, however, that risk is worth the exposure to it. In virtually every case I have studied, churches lose more people to neglect than to schism. Churches that fail to legitimize lay ministry inevitably experience a steady stream of people falling through the cracks.

Churches that fail to legitimize lay ministry inevitably experience a steady stream of people falling through the cracks.

If you properly care for your leaders, you will not lose as many people to schism as you do to neglect. Most churches routinely lose half their newest people through neglect; you won't lose 1% to schism if the pastoral staff is routinely listening to its leaders. Being a good listener builds loyalty and love. That's how you *show* you care. That's how people *know* you care.

No researcher or Bible teacher has found a guaranteed way of "schism-proofing" a church. Neglect and fallaway can be promised. However, you will lose more out the "back door" than you will ever lose to schism.

God's new, after-Pentecost strategy deals with people in handfuls as well as by hundreds. Those ordained clergy following the "pre-Jethro paradigm" lead by hundreds, while lay leaders following the "Book of Acts paradigm" work by house-to-house groups of about ten. When you add up the harvest being reached, often those who lead hundreds wear out by the time they get to thousands. Lay people who lead by tens are still looking for more people to help when the overall totals surpass tens of thousands.

God's new after-Pentecost strategy deals with people in handfuls rather than by hundreds.

A great dividing line was crossed at Jesus' ascension. It needs to be recognized that by His Spirit there is now virtually no limit to the supply of lay ministers He will make available in a church.

Acts of Serving Lead to Healthy Churches

The more I work with small-group leaders, the more aware I become of the fact that these people can become the key to the health of a congregation. It is true that they help produce attendance for the worship services. Years ago, in churches where the Sunday school movement was in its heyday, pastors knew that a strong program of Sunday school classes would account for some 80% of the worship attendance. Putting emphasis there would build the overall church.

Today that principle is just as true. Given the rise of many types of groups in churches—worship teams, home Bible studies, support groups, etc.—today it takes a strong *overall* system of groups to build a church's worship attendance, as Key Six explained.

Thus, from an organizational point of view, it's important that the small groups and ministry teams of a congregation make their work available to help the church run its ministries and programs. But even more important is an all-pervasive attitude of service as part of maturity in Christ. Most Christians, because of the batterings we receive in life, tend at one time or another to withdraw into ourselves and become a little defensive and guarded. As we develop stronger habits of serving, both in the group and one-on-one, we will find new ways to touch the lives of others. This is where the act of serving becomes a critically important component of Christian growth.

From the standpoint of Christian spiritual growth, it's important that you as a group leader put your people in an environment where they see that it makes sense to give themselves away to other people. Some of that serving will benefit the church as an organized religious body, but some of it will go far beyond the organized, on-premises programs of the church. It will go to people wherever they are hurting, both those within the church and those outside.

In the act of serving we become more kind and gracious people one to another, on premises, and out in the community. There is great power in serving.

Unmet Needs Are Present in Your Group

Serving starts and is most spontaneous in the context of the needs disclosed in a small group. In our home we have a house rule that says we give appropriate notice before promising to entertain someone. I had grown up in a home where my mother's gift of hospitality was such that she thrilled to feed a dozen guests on a moment's notice. Then I married into a family that entertained formally. As part of our marriage, I learned to be a responsible inviter by respecting my wife's culture of making time for formal preparation. Typically, when the opportunity for hospitality arises,

How to Serve #3: Listen carefully for personal needs disclosed in your group which you can meet.

146

my wife normally prefers an hour or so to work through issues relating to childcare, shopping, schedule conflicts, and the like.

I was sitting one night in a small group with my wife Grace on my left and an intern at the nearby medical school on my right. His third child was about to be born and his wife had gone back to her mother's town to give birth, as was the custom in their culture. Given his rigorous hospital schedule, that seemed to be the most sensible option.

The latest cause for prayer, he explained, was that he had a 72-hour rotation beginning the next day at the university medical center. His childcare plans for their teenage daughter had fallen through just before he came to the meeting. He confessed his concern for his daughter being home alone all weekend and said he didn't know what to do about it.

He had barely finished describing the challenge when Grace reached over, touched his arm, and said, "We'll take her." Grace is one of the most organized people I know. She doesn't do hospitality casually. I knew she hadn't had time to process all the implications of her statement. By saying yes, she spontaneously authorized a complete disruption of her weekend.

I sensed that something unusual was taking place.

He said, "You would?"

"Sure," she replied.

The man breathed a sign of relief. He indicated his appreciation that we were meeting a real need in his life. They compared schedules and then Grace agreed to pick up the daughter at 5:30 the next afternoon.

When Grace picked up the girl, they hit it off immediately. They prepared dinner together and seemed to be having a wonderful mother-daughter kind of a time.

As the evening grew later, I became tired and went to bed. Meanwhile Grace and this teen kept talking. At 4:30 in the morning, someone disturbed my sleep. It was Grace, climbing into bed. "Are you okay?" I asked, "It's 4:30!"

"I know," she replied. "This girl needed a mother to talk to tonight. She didn't stop talking until just now."

I saw my wife operating under obviously what was the impulse of the Spirit. Without the trust and love that are characteristic of a healthy small group, it would be very difficult to arrange something as intimate to a family's well-being as the care of a child for an overnighter under such short notice.

Heartfelt Service Can't Be Bought

Could our friend have hired someone to listen to his teenage daughter from 5:30 in the afternoon until 4:30 in the morning? That help is generally not available for sale, even from my wife who has stayed up many a night with our own six children, not to mention litters of newborn puppies that we have raised. Rather, genuine heart-felt service wells up as God's love touches from one person to another, making the gospel credible and the Body of Christ tangible.

Can you imagine the medical student standing up in the middle of his church's worship service? "Excuse me, I've got a teenager staying at home alone, would someone please pray for us?" That wouldn't seem appropriate in many cases. You need the intimacy of a small-group to disclose that level of need, and people must be close enough to reach out and touch the need and say, "Let's make it happen."

You need the intimacy of a small-group to disclose that level of need.

In situations like these, the Holy Spirit is so present that they become known as sacred moments. "The love of Christ was so real that night," people will remember. "It was a precious thing. We're all heartwarmed when we think about it." Yet all that happened was a simple act of kindness.

How to Serve #4:

Begin to extend acts of serving to people beyond your group.

A Contagious Climate of Giving

If we establish a pattern of serving one another in the group, then extending love and care to other people is a fairly natural next step. When you see someone struggling with home repairs, children with problems at school, a need to be picked up at the car-repair shop and so forth, you can follow the same habit that you've developed in your group.

You will say, "I had a great experience in a similar situation in my small group. I wonder what would happen if I offer to help here, too." As you leave the group, you begin to look for ways individually to do random acts of kindness.

I have some friends who began to experiment with this concept. They'd pay the food order for the person behind them at a McDonald's drive through or they'd feed people's parking meters. They discovered it was more fun to throw money at people than to throw it away in self-serving activities. Who knows what good will come of it? These ideas sometimes sound crazy, but at times God clearly leads a believer or group to do these things. Thus we establish a climate of giving, and it extends to the church missions program, to care and relief programs overseas, and even to a willingness personally to go out on mission ourselves.

Not only do you want people to model giving to one another, and also beyond themselves, but how about taking your whole group into a serving mode? Maybe they could relieve the ushers or babysitting crew for one of the church's ministries. Perhaps they could volunteer to join the church trustees in cleaning up the playground area. The idea here is for a caring, Bible study-type group to become a task group for temporary service.

I know of one church in a certain town that had scheduled a very important all-church meeting. The evening's discussion and decision would impact how their future related to their denomination. Another church down the street, hearing of the situation, contacted them and said, "Our people would like to volunteer to cover the childcare so that all your adults can attend the plenary gathering. That Sunday afternoon, when you meet together, our Christian education workers will be here in our facility and will gladly watch your church's children during your meeting."

Acts of kindness touch lives and move hearts.

These churches weren't even part of the same denomination, but 10 years later the pastors are still telling the story. Acts of kindness touch lives and move hearts.

A particular group in a church can be mobilized as well, asking "What could we do on occasion that would be helpful?" Help in Communion? Costuming for the choir? (Those groups who are "chartered" as task groups, such as sports teams or sound technicians, could profit from doing just the opposite: scheduling withdrawal time to love each other, to fellowship, and to do Bible study together).

What opportunities are available to lead your group into service? Certainly there's a place for keeping the church's ministries going. Virtually all churches produce large-group worship services. These times of corporate worship provide many opportunities for service, such as through artistic and musical talent, decorations, Christian education, mission booths, etc. Similarly, a church's age-specialized groups are constantly in search of volunteer help.

What would happen to the scoutmaster, AWANA leader, or divorce-recovery support group if someone came up and asked, "May our small group provide special refreshments for the staff and children next Wednesday night? We'll give your workers a break." What kind of boost would occur?

Serving Crosses Cultures for Christ

Sometimes groups partner together in serving projects, with the weaker groups benefiting from the presence of the stronger groups. In urban areas where evangelism sometimes accompanies group formations, members of strong groups will go to the neighborhoods where a weak group is holding evangelistic meetings. They'll meet the neighbors and friends of the locally based group, try to find new prospects, and visit on the group's behalf.

On other occasions churches will use teams in cross-cultural ministry. Most churches have neighbors living near their facilities who are not of the same culture as the people who attend the church. If your church houses only "your kind" of people, then perhaps one of your church's cells can come alongside an embryo Christian group of another culture, assisting, serving, and ministering with them until enough leaders can be discipled in that culture.

As such your church can become a sponsor of satellite organizations, groups, and classes cross-culturally. Due to language, cultural distinctives or other concerns, people from that culture might not be comfortable simply walking into your church facility and joining the majority group.

Maybe, however, they would appreciate the use of space in your buildings for meetings in their language, for events suitable for their youth, or for follow-up of those they've led to faith in Christ. Your group might serve as a hosting group by providing refreshments, supporting in the development of one or more satellite services for language groups and people of other cultures. Your group might serve as a liaison with a language group to ensure their continual welcome within your facilities, becoming an advocate in the inevitable conflicts and disputes that arise. In doing so, you'll be contributing to a missionary effort right at home.

It used to be that you had to take a group across the state line or out of the country for them to feel like missionaries. Many people can tell stories of how such trips initially catalyzed their own calls to serving. Today, most North American cities have dozens if not hundreds of cultures and languages represented. Bridging into these nearby cultures becomes an opportunity.

A Simple Tool for Identifying Spiritual Gifts

As you seek God's guidance about where to take your group for serving and what to do, examine two issues closely. First, what spiritual gifts do your people bring? If you don't have the gifts compatible with a particular kind of serving, your group may become discouraged.

How to Serve #5: Combine spiritual gifts and serving to build bridges and win a hearing for Christ.

Every description of crisis that comes into the group will receive a response according to the spiritual giftedness of the people sitting around the circle. Some will analyze, some will direct, some will move in close, some will comfort, some will instruct.

I've often conducted an exercise by telling groups of a true, life-threatening experience I had. On a flight coming into New York's LaGuardia airport, the plane hit some of the worse turbulence I'd ever experienced. We were just offshore, circling a section of the Atlantic

Ocean and unable to find a break in the clouds. Things went from bad to worse and the flight attendants instructed us to assume crash positions. The cabin was silent as we watched the frame of the plane twisting and writhing. You could look down the aisle, and see the line of overhead racks twist and snake as the fuselage contorted.

The pilot aborted one landing attempt and then a second. Whispered conversations began that were decidedly muted and spiritual in character. Earlier in the flight, I had talked about spiritual things with my seat mates; now our conversation became very somber and intense.

Everyone aboard was facing the fact that in just a few minutes, all of us might be at the bottom of the ocean floor. My prayer was this: "Lord, if these are my last moments here on this earth, what should I think about, pray, or do?" My next thought was...

At this point, I stop telling my story and ask those I'm addressing how they'd fill in the next sentence if they had been aboard. One by one my hearers said:

- "I'd stand up and say, 'Receive Christ while there's time!'"
- "All those people on the ground; they'll be brokenhearted."
- "I'd pray, 'God give the pilot wisdom and let the tower know how to advise him.'"

Every time I've conducted this exercise, those participating can discern the analyst, comforter, administrator, evangelist, and pastor in the comments. All of us have a different response, each of which was indicative of our spiritual giftedness.

Thus if you're not sure whether the giftedness of your group would be appropriate for a particular serving opportunity, simply describe the circumstances and ask, "If you were there, what would you do?" The responses of your group members will give you some of your best clues as to what gifts are in operation.

Second, be sure to consider the backgrounds represented in your group. For example, is one of your people Filipino? Or has one of your members worked in the Philippines? If so, perhaps that person has contacts and trust within the Filipino community. Often the opportunities God guides us to take will emerge within the context of the background and connections of the people already present in the group. Most times you don't need a special manual (other than the

Bible); you simply need to build on the webs of influence represented by people's connections. Simply follow their interests and leanings, asking, "What can we do to support you?"

Often the opportunities God guides us to take will emerge within the context of the background and connections of the people already present in the group.

Your group can provide an amazing amount of support to a wide variety of needs! It will become another point of light, another place of serving that can enlarge the kingdom. Service in Jesus' name can build bridges and win a hearing for Christ.

A small group leader in the Midwest told me about a fellow named Ken who had lots of needs. Ken was so angry with God that he had ripped up every Bible in his home and thrown them in the trash. He was depressed even to the point of considering suicide.

One night, after months of invitations, he came to the group my friend leads. The people there listened to him, encouraged him, and accepted him. They used their gifts to serve his needs, both in and outside the group. Over a six-month period Ken's life stabilized.

"I can see dramatic changes in Ken's life every week," my friend reports. "His faith is being strengthened so much that he is now turning to others in the group, and helping them with *their* needs."

It's sobering to think of what happens in a church where there isn't a small group to catch a person like him. Where would he go? My friend's congregation has experienced a new boldness and energy in direct proportion to their willingness to give their lives away in caring for other people.

A mature small group will devote as serious an attention to serving as they do to worship. Why? Because part of God's plan for His people involves worship through serving. For example, at some point you may decide to go as a team to preach and minister in the jail.

If you offer the words to the gospel of Christ without the Body of Christ, it will have no life-changing power for most people. The words

153

of the gospel are designed to be accompanied by loving people. That's what serving can do as your group reaches beyond your borders.

The words to the gospel of Christ without the Body of Christ ...have no life-changing power for most people.

Don't fail to take advantage of the privilege of effective volunteer ministry.

W<small>IN</small>

Connect: Build a strong link with the pastoral
staff.

Recruit: Keep your leadership nucleus fresh and
growing.

Invite: Cultivate a larger contact group through
enthusiasm and care.

Prepare: Tailor a plan that you can prayerfully
personalize to your group and
apprentices.

Meet: Convene your group in such a way that
people genuinely experience the Body
of Christ.

Bring: Help each group member appreciate the
whole church through larger corporate
worship.

Serve: Make time to serve needs in and beyond
the group.

**Win: Initiate the kind of outreach that
makes Christ real to people.**

Seek:

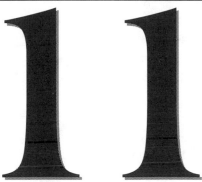

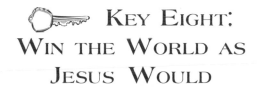 KEY EIGHT:
WIN THE WORLD AS
JESUS WOULD

CHAPTER SUMMARY

How to Win:

☑ 1. Notice what the Holy Spirit is already doing.

☑ 2. Be willing to respond to opportunities for telling your story and Jesus' story.

☑ 3. Learn how to use Scripture to support the truths of your story.

☑ 4. Exercise faith for the people God will bring your way.

☑ 5. Ask God to show you two unbelieving persons who are struggling.

YOU AND I ARE THE HANDS, FEET, AND EARS OF JESUS CHRIST to our own generation, touching people where Jesus would if He were here in person. It is the privilege of small groups to be part of what God is doing to redeem and reconcile a sinful world to Himself.

157

Most small group leaders don't realize that small groups are becoming the most effective entry port to the Christian faith worldwide. As this chapter will explain, doing "the work of an evangelist" (2 Timothy 4:5) is more often accomplished in a small group than through any other role in a church.

Doing "the work of an evangelist" (2 Timothy 4:5) is more often accomplished in a small group than through any other role in a church.

If these statements are true, then perhaps something hasn't been appreciated about the nature of small groups. Your role as a small group leader is related to a powerful secret of the expansion of the Christian movement!

Observations Across North America

During my consulting ministry, I stumbled across something very significant on one of my visits to Edmonton, Alberta. Most of my experience and research up to that point had been with clergy, but due to an unusual series of events, a number of small-group leaders showed up to this meeting as well.

How to Win #1: Notice what the Holy Spirit is already doing.

Before I began speaking on the pre-assigned topic of evangelism, an idea popped into my head—which later I interpreted as a nudge from the Lord—to ask, "How many group leaders in this room have seen adults in your groups come to faith in Christ within the last 12 months?" I was amazed to see one fourth of the hands go up. I further learned that within those groups signified by raised hands, more than half had seen *more* than one conversion.

This idea of people coming to faith through small groups had been advanced to me a year earlier during an interview with the founding pastor of a church that receives 10,000 adult converts from Buddhism each month. (No, that five-digit number is *not* a typo. It's ten thousand!) He and I were involved in a series of meetings in South Africa. At one point he commented to me over breakfast, "You know, our church doesn't evangelize the way you do in the United States."

"How?" I asked, "do you win 120,000 or more to Christ in a year?"

"One at a time," he replied. "We have many cell groups in our church. I have asked the group leaders to do the work of an evangelist. Every cell group leader first wins a hearing for the gospel." They don't begin with a verbal witness. Rather they win a hearing by acts of love, serving, and kindness.

He continued: "I instruct my cell group leaders to look around their workplace and neighborhood. They are to find someone who is struggling at some point." He explained that the struggle could be as modest as not being able to get a load of groceries up to their apartment for lack of someone to hold the elevator door open. Or it could be a shopkeeper with a need, even as simple as for sweeping his floor. Perhaps the children in a family need after-school tutoring.

He commented further. "I tell my small group leaders to help them. Structure your life, carving out time to be with that person. Be there and offer assistance. Do this on a consistent basis until they ask, 'Why are you treating me so well?' At this point you may say, 'I am a servant of Jesus Christ, and He's told me to do good to all people. I saw you struggling and as I prayed, I knew that if Jesus were here, He would help you."

"Why is this approach effective?" I asked.

"What this does is to eliminate people's resistance to the gospel." my colleague continued. "From that point on, I tell them, they will ask questions and you can share your personal faith, invite them to your cell group, and bring them to church with you." My friend indicated that from the time group leaders have someone in their heart that they begin to serve until that newcomer is in the church as a baptized member is typically four months. On average, then, each group leader can extend love and service to two people a year with room to spare.

This pastor's name is David Yonggi Cho and the church he leads is in Seoul, Korea. His bottom-line discovery is that you don't have to be a high-powered public evangelist in order to invite people to give their lives to Jesus. When a heart is ready to receive the Word, as long as the message is understandable, people can receive it because they've been prepared. They are like fertile soil that God has readied for seed to take root and grow. Serving is the tool for soil preparation.

Serving is the tool for soil preparation.

Dr. Cho went on his way, and I pondered what his comments meant. They expressed such a simple concept, but I didn't know what to do with it. Then in Edmonton I first discovered that this same process was happening in North America in an unpublicized way.

My next travels took me to Denver, so I conducted a similar survey with the same findings. The results were identical in Chicago at the next stop. In short, everywhere I went for the next several months I learned that already, spontaneously, about one fourth of the typical church's groups were seeing life change in people at the level of conversion.

About one fourth of the typical church's groups were seeing life change in people at the level of conversion.

The Pattern Within Small Groups

I then begin asking small group leaders to tell stories about how people had come to faith in the context of the small group. Most had a familiar ring: contact, love shown, concern and interest, and bridges built at the social level. Sooner or later an opportunity emerged for the gospel to be voiced. Hearers would respond by indicating a desire to receive Christ.

I also began noting the ethnic background of group leaders who were giving testimony. They covered the range of races and tribes—Anglo, African, Asian. In subsequent years, I've seen the same principles work everywhere from Cincinnati, Ohio to London, England. It seems that God is beginning to move through small groups in all kinds of churches to bring people to faith in Christ.

Over time, I've learned that if I want to receive God's blessing, then I should align myself with something He's doing. That's a far better approach than coming up with my own ideas and asking Him to bless them.

If I want to receive God's blessing, then I should align myself with something He's doing.

The most important question to ask is, "Lord what are *You* up to?" Then I try to join what I understand to be His agenda. In this case, He seems to want His followers to be willing to be used to prepare a heart for the gospel. What a joy to be an instrument of the Holy Spirit in building bridges to people whom God is drawing to Himself!

If you are willing to participate in what the Holy Spirit is already doing, then the "human agency" side of your job is to ask for discernment. Seek God for who can be served, search out that person, and structure time in your life to assist him or her. In so doing you may well win a hearing for the gospel.

If you do the seeking and serving part, you can leave the "conversion" part to God, as long as you are willing to tell your story.

Simple Ways to Tell Your Story

John Soper, who lives in New Jersey, has started dozens of small groups in his life. Many of them begin with a study in the Gospel of Mark. As soon as possible he leads the group to examine the story of the demon-possessed man whom Jesus heals. His life dramatically changed, this man who lived among the tombstones tries to stop Jesus from leaving. He begs Jesus for permission to go with him. The Bible says, "Jesus did not let him, but said, 'Go home to your family and tell them how much the Lord has done for you, and how he has had mercy on you'" (Mark 5:19, NIV).

> *How to Win #2: Be willing to respond to opportunities for telling your story and Jesus' story.*

Based on this story my friend John proposes this simple sequence for Christians in telling their story:

• You saw what I was.
• You see what I am.
• Jesus made the difference.
• Are you interested?

After you've won a hearing from someone, you need to be able to tell your story, describing how you came to faith in Jesus Christ. "Always be ready to give a reason for the hope within you," commands the Scripture (see 1 Peter 3:15). You must do so in a way that is not confusing. You may first want to practice with friends, describing how you came to understand your need for Christ and how you received Him. What truth came to your attention, in what way, leading you to bow to Jesus Christ as Savior and Lord? How is your life different today?

Don't Omit the Acquaintance Process

In telling your story, you may find it helpful to describe the path of how God brought you to faith in Jesus Christ as well as the path God used to bring you into community with other believers. For some people the intertwining of those paths is inseparable. Others tend to separate out and recount only the parts about how they were reconciled with God.

The conviction process brings us from our current lost condition to the cross of Jesus Christ because He is God the Father's provision for our sins. A point of faith comes, our forgiveness is received, and our conversion is effected.

The acquaintance path brings us into the Christian fold as a part of the Body of Christ. We move from being a loner to being among the family of God. This process leads people to join a small group or church.

Both pathways and processes are important to a new believer's ongoing spiritual health.

Identify a Biblical Foundation for Your Faith

How to Win #3: Learn how to use Scripture to support the truths of your story.

You also need to be able to express a Biblical basis for the claims you're making. You need to know something of the passages of Scripture that describe God's plan of deliverance. A good starting point is to meditate on and memorize John 3:16 or Romans 10:9-10. However, the longer you're involved in leading groups, the more you should know about how to be a witness and how to explain the relevant Bible passages.

Are you aware, for example, that the Bible uses at least three major image systems to present God's salvation? Jesus' teaching was so understandable because He based it on stories involving commonplace objects and ideas—flowers of the field, yeast that expands, houses built upon sand, and bushes that need pruning. Similarly, the Bible's story of "holy history" uses powerful word pictures that invite ready comprehension for those who are seeking.

For example, Scripture presents a tribal system that leads to a kingdom. God brought the Jewish nation into existence, and then He brought Christ to that Jewish nation as well as to the whole world.

There is also a courtroom image that shows the justification process. Jesus Christ is presented as the God-man who pays the penalty of sinners.

There is a family analogy, where those who believe are made to become children of God.

If you can place these word pictures within the reach of people so they can see God's intentions to bring salvation through Jesus Christ, then you are Biblically prepared to do the work of evangelization.

Set a Simple, Reachable Goal

Goals release faith. They enable you to say, "What would happen if..." or "If God is in this thing, where might it lead?" or "If God's will were perfectly expressed in the ministry of this group, would there be an evangelistic outcome?" Good goals involve risk as you ask yourself, "Do we dare open ourselves to that kind of potential response?"

How to Win #4: Exercise faith for the people God will bring your way.

Whatever kind of group you lead, there are people within the influence of your group's membership who are wide open to the most wonderful, liberating, life-changing good news in the universe (even if they're scared or turned off from churches). If you believe that statement, then the next step is to pray: "God, more than anything else, I want to do what you are blessing." Don't be surprised if the Holy Spirit prompts you in response, as He already seems to be communicating to others, "Then do the work of an evangelist."

Here's the kind of commitment necessary to make if you want to do evangelism through your group: I offer myself to be used by God to show His love to friends and neighbors who are not yet following Jesus Christ. During the next 12 months, I will ask God to guide me to two unbelieving persons who are struggling, and will make time to serve them out of my love for God, as expressed in His desire that Christians should "do good to all." I will make this matter an ongoing prayer in my small group, and will be ready to explain that my motivation to serve begins with God's loving provisions for humanity: "We love because He first loved us."

You Don't Need to Be a Gifted Evangelist

The phrase, "Do the work of an evangelist" (2 Timothy 2:5), is one of the most important and releasing concepts in the New Testament. By analogy, you may not have the spiritual gift of "teaching" (Romans 12:7), but you can still "teach and admonish one another" (Colossians 3:16) with your group. You may not have the spiritual gift of "serving" (Romans 12:7), but you can still "serve one another in love" (Galatians 5:13) and "offer hospitality to one another" (1 Peter 4:9). You may not have the gift of "contributing to the needs of others" (Romans 12:8), but you and all other believers can still give "generously ...and ...cheerfully ...on every occasion" (2 Corinthians 9:6-11).

The gift of evangelism is not required to win people to Christ. Rather your most important contribution is a willingness to serve people in love as an agent of Jesus. Such pastoral care will not be limited to people who are already in the fold, but will also go to those whom God is drawing into faith.

Therefore no longer does anyone have to say, "I can't do gospel ministry because I don't have the gift of an evangelist." If you have a new life in Christ, then you have something to say and the privilege of voicing it. The woman at the well had been converted for only a few minutes when she "went back to the town and said to the people, 'Come ...could this be the Christ?'" (John 4:28-29). Whether you're a newcomer to the faith or a mature Christian, you can play a part in a global movement of evangelism. Doing the work of the evangelist is what the Holy Spirit is ready to bless next.

Doing the work of the evangelist is what the Holy Spirit is ready to bless next.

A New Era for Evangelistic Opportunity

The joy of watching God win souls is a privilege of being the leader of a small group. When you first think about calling together a group of people who can learn to love one another and obey the Christian gospel, you may not have the winning of people to Jesus Christ and His truth as one of your objectives, but it is still one of your great privileges.

One reason many churches don't experience high conversion rates is that we have not taken seriously enough the charge to do the work of an evangelist. We've not put God's evangelistic commission in the hands of the right people. If we organize our churches so that the smallest units—the classes, teams, cells, and other small groups—are seen as the place where people can meet God and each other, and from there come together for large-group worship, then we will become conversion-oriented churches.

We've not put God's evangelistic commission in the hands of the right people.

Christianity has the ability to touch people who were not born within the context of the Christian faith, but yet allows them the full privilege of the Gospel, including the reconciliation made possible by the death of Jesus Christ, the forgiveness of sins, the promise of eternal life, the love and peace of God, and the companionship of other believers on the way. These dramatic life changes, open to all who believe, have made Christianity the most important religious influence in the history of the world.

What Would Jesus Do?

So the group leader's challenge is this: part of your task is to organize your time in such a way, with enough simplicity, that you have time to

165

love someone who doesn't "deserve" love. Your goal can be as basic as saying the following: "I will serve whomever God puts in my path."

How to Win #5: Ask God to show you two unbelieving persons who are struggling.

What shape will serving take? All you have to do as a Christian is to ask: "If this were Jesus standing here, what would He do? How would He show love? How would he teach? How would He encourage?" Then simply behave like that—as empowered by the Holy Spirit. If you do, God can use you mightily as an agent for His kingdom.

Ask, "If this were Jesus standing here, what would He do?" ...Then simply behave like that as empowered by the Holy Spirit.

The Importance of the Group

Conversion is truly the work of God. He invites us to play a part as He loves people through us. That atmosphere of care, acceptance, and listening, when surrounded by prayer, puts people in a frame of heart and mind to hear what we're trying to say. Our first step is to win a hearing in the acquaintance process. In the process, the Holy Spirit's conviction is greatly accelerated in many cases.

The small group offers a safe place for people to receive love. Then, when they have come among you and they see the larger Christian community, you can interpret what they are observing or hearing about: a baptism, a special class taught by the pastor, other "next steps" of obedience and maturity. You will also put them in a mode that makes it the most natural thing in the world for them to turn around, become your apprentice, find someone struggling like they were, go out and get alongside that person—and you've just created a means by which many can come to faith in Christ as the Holy Spirit nudges, draws, and calls people into the grace of God.

Not Every Group Will Seize This Opportunity

Which groups in your church are the ones most likely to play a role in evangelism? The newest groups commissioned are typically the ones

166

most likely to accept a charter for a "new" way of doing evangelism. Not knowing any better, it often doesn't occur to them to "departmentalize" evangelism or discipleship to another arena of the church.

Many existing groups don't have supervision or apprentice training in place, and so it's much harder to change their culture. Announcements from the pulpit and other fanfare intended to invite groups to develop an evangelistic culture usually have the opposite effect. Existing groups typically respond better to role models of successful accomplishment ("Tammy's group reports another conversion—let's ask God for that kind of response throughout the church!") rather than to premature announcements of intent ("We're asking all groups to try something new").

Existing groups typically respond better to role models of successful accomplishment ...rather than to premature announcements of intent.

In many existing churches, a three to four year period of culture shift is necessary for new groups to model a partnership in evangelism and for existing groups to open themselves to reaching out, winning a hearing, and sharing the gospel in the context of community.

Sometimes, however, the response is immediate because receptive hearts have already been prepared. For instance, a young group leader named Trevor accepted the challenge to make space in his life for someone unchurched and unbelieving. He offered God his recreational tennis as a way to befriend others. Trevor prayed that God would use tennis as His means of drawing someone to Himself.

Through an unusual series of events, a church member phoned Trevor and said, "I have a friend whose son is looking for a tennis partner. I hear that you play."

Trevor placed a call to the son, Mike. "It was the most awkward call I'd made in my life," Trevor reports. "But he was warm to me and we had a good time playing tennis."

Trevor found out that his new friend's birthday was coming up in a couple of weeks. That week, in the small group Trevor leads, he asked the members, "Would we be willing to take this guy out to dinner for his birthday?"

The group followed through on the suggestion and Mike seemed to enjoy meeting them. Trevor continued to play tennis with Mike. "I was too immature to initiate a conversation about Mike's need for the Savior," Trevor says, "but for three months, I prayed daily for his conversion."

One Saturday, after Trevor and Mike had played tennis in a tournament together, Mike asked to go to church with Trevor. Then a couple of weeks later Mike asked if he could come to one of the group meetings that Trevor leads. "He liked it and asked a lot of questions," reports Trevor. "I saw him pray for the first time. A month later, he prayed to receive Christ."

The story doesn't end there, however. "Now he's coming regularly to church and he's brought a non-Christian friend to the group," reports Trevor. "It's amazing what happens when you pray and don't give up."

"...but for three months, I prayed daily for his conversion ...It's amazing what happens when you pray and don't give up."

God used Trevor and his home group as a side door into the faith and into the fellowship of the church. All this wonderful activity occurred within a year of Trevor opening his life to make time for others. "It's been so exciting to see how God has used the group to help Mike come to know the Lord," says Trevor.

Do you suppose that over the next year you, too, could make space for this kind of outreach? What if you asked God to show you someone in whom you should invest relational time? Will you make yourself available so that God might use your presence as a door to faith—a way of drawing someone to the Savior? If you'll take that first step, the Holy Spirit will do His work from there.

What are you willing to do in response to the Lord?

Evangelism with After-Care Built In
Without anyone's announcement of a national campaign, with no

evangelist's face or name on it, the Holy Spirit has started routinely bringing people to faith in Christ in one group in four, whether or not evangelism is an announced goal of that group.

We may be seeing the beginning of an outpouring in our era; this "new" door of evangelism may be the most important phenomena of our times. The significance is that it doesn't merely ask for a nod to the gospel and its words, leaving someone without the certainty of care. Rather, group-based evangelism proceeds from the nurture and shepherding ministry of caring groups that are already attached to a worshiping church community.

This "new" door of evangelism may be the most important phenomena of our times.

Thus when people come to the gospel they're coming to Christ in the form of His church through groups where pastoral care is already in place. To use a hospital analogy, the follow-up is arranged in the pre-op stage, so people are already being loved when they become converted.

The follow-up is done in the pre-op stage, so people are already being loved when they become converted.

Do you believe God will use you and your group to do the work of an evangelist? If so, then you will be part of winning the world as Jesus would—doing what Jesus would do if He were here in His physical body with you.

Are you now ready to voice your resolve to God? The following prayer is a guideline you might use. Take some time to declare God's goodness and greatness (Key Six) and then make this resolution before Him: "Lord, for the next 12 months I will ask you to show me two people with needs in my neighborhood or workplace to whom I can extend kindness in Jesus' name to the end that they can hear the gospel. When they ask me why I am serving them, I will explain that, 'I love Jesus, He loves you, and He wants me to help you. This help comes from someone bigger than me.'"

May God help you as you make this commitment and then as you search out someone to begin serving. May you be aware of the Holy Spirit's presence and may you see much fruit.

SEEK

Connect: Build a strong link with the pastoral staff.

Recruit: Keep your leadership nucleus fresh and growing.

Invite: Cultivate a larger contact group through enthusiasm and care.

Prepare: Tailor a plan that you can prayerfully personalize to your group and apprentices.

Meet: Convene your group in such a way that people genuinely experience the Body of Christ.

Bring: Help each group member appreciate the whole church through larger corporate worship.

Serve: Make time to serve needs in and beyond the group.

Win: Initiate the kind of outreach that makes Christ real to people.

 Seek: Experience the renewal of God's strength as you regularly meet with Him in secret.

CHAPTER

12

🔑 KEY NINE:
SEEK GOD'S RENEWAL AS YOU
MEET HIM IN SECRET

CHAPTER SUMMARY

How to Seek:
☑ 1. Recognize the value of a secret life with God
through Christ.
☑ 2. Make time for solitude.
☑ 3. Be part of a small-group community.
☑ 4. Maintain a lifestyle charactcrized by simplicity.
☑ 5. Exercise faith.

EVERYONE LOVES A SECRET—ESPECIALLY IF IT'S SOMEONE
else's. Magazines with titles like *People, Gossip, Profiles,* and
Inside Perspective are popular because human beings like to
learn about each other. We're curious about what makes others tick or
what high-visibility people do in their private lives. Sometimes we see
strong character underneath; sometimes we're disappointed to find
only an emptiness and hollowness.

Someone has said, "Character is who we are when we think no one else is looking." In our walk with God, there's a direct relation between what we do in those "secret" moments and who we become in public.

A staff pastor once said to me, "Do you see this young woman? For eight weeks in a row people promised to come to her small group, and no one showed up. After the first week, she came to me shattered. I encouraged her to remain in prayer, and she decided to try it again. The second and third weeks passed, each with the same dismal results. After eight weeks of no-shows, the group took off. She developed one of the finest, strongest, and most evangelistic groups in the church. And yet she couldn't get the first person to attend until she had been spurned eight times, with her and an apprentice being left with a plateful of cookies to eat by themselves."

That young lady and her apprentice knew how to seek God! What do you suppose was going on when a normal, sane, friendly person couldn't get an attendance week after week? She was effective in inviting friends out to lunch or to church. All the obvious signs predicted success in the launch of this new group.

A spiritual battle must have been taking place because it seemed like the gates of hell finally yielded. Gates are defensive structures built to hold you out when you want to go in. Jesus said they could not prevail against the advance of His kingdom (see Matthew 16:18). If you are advancing in your ministry toward people who need God's love, only to find that they can't respond to you, then your work is being blocked. Gates don't move to attack you; they sit there waiting to be overcome. It's as we pray in the secret place, seek God's will, and ask Him for release, that God promises to reward openly.

You want to see lives changed and people encouraged? Then follow the eight Keys previously described in this book:

1. *Connect* with the leadership network in your church
2. *Recruit* a leader-in-training
3. *Invite* newcomers to your group
4. *Prepare* for the group to meet
5. *Meet* together for ministry
6. *Bring* your group to worship
7. *Serve* the group and others beyond
8. *Win* the world as Jesus would

Then in your secret place, tell God, "I want to see Your glory in my life as I see their lives changed. I'm not going to stop asking until I get it. Jesus said, I should ask, seek, knock, and that's what I'm doing."

I have never known a Christian who followed that procedure only to find that God wasn't willing or able to keep His end of the bargain. If you take care of the secret stuff, all else will break open in its own time.

If you take care of the secret stuff, all else will break open in its own time.

Bible Greats Reveal Powerful Prayer Lives

Wouldn't it be wonderful if the most significant secret in your life were the same as that of Daniel of old? He is the second most powerful man in his nation. His adversaries, seeking for an opportunity to trip him up, look for a scandal in his life. They soon catch on that Daniel's secret is prayer. As they spy on him in secret, they learn that the man who manages one of the largest nations of his era is more loyal to his God than to his king. He prays even

How to Seek #1: Recognize the value of a secret life with God through Christ.

when prayer is not legally permitted. His reliability and trustworthiness is based on a loyalty to Someone even higher than the king.

Daniel illustrates something Jesus says: the things you do in secret will be revealed publicly. Jesus presented a paradox, saying in effect, "You want to be known for something? Have a secret." The secret is your communion with God (see Matthew 6:4-18 and the Book of Daniel). You can't keep it secret, but you should nevertheless have a secret life. No matter how little you say publicly about your secret walk, the consequences cannot be hidden over time. It etches itself in your face and shows up in the blessings God brings into your life.

Your secret walk ...shows up in the blessings God brings into your life.

175

I have at various times been compulsive, workaholic, overextended, exasperated, worn out, burned out, and fatigued. As that driven lifestyle took its toll on my body, doctors discovered a cancer requiring the removal of one of my adrenal glands.

Was there a relationship between the two? Medical authorities aren't agreed whether excessive adrenaline usage can be cause-and-effect linked to various health maladies. Yet it still troubled me to think that perhaps my cancer stemmed from my being so high on body-made chemicals. My adrenaline addiction secrets were no longer hidden!

A rather well-to-do businessman in a Midwestern city has some 400 employees, many of whom are members of the Teamsters Union. He told me of a time when the government began conducting random tests for drug use in an effort to crack down on chemical abuse among truck drivers. Almost everywhere the federal investigators went, their tests uncovered one in five drivers as an active drug user.

One day the government showed up at my friend's business. However, the inspectors couldn't find a single violation. They were so surprised that they even checked to see if fraud was occurring at the laboratory level.

I happen to know that my friend has a secret life. His secret life is not that of bribing laboratories, but being prayerfully concerned for the welfare of his drivers. Christian or otherwise, they are constantly under the protection of this man's fervent prayer. So are his other business decisions. The results are so noticeable that even government inspectors are stymied. "Why don't you have the 'normal' number of drug users among your employees?" they marvel.

Do you want to have a powerful ministry and be a blessing to people? If so, then develop a secret life. Seek God's renewal as you meet Him in secret.

How to Seek #2: Make time for solitude.

You Need Times of Solitude

What's involved in developing an effective secret in the area of spiritual growth? I remember one time when a man slipped into the back row of some meetings I was leading. Later he came up and identified himself as being in private practice as a

Christian counselor. He gave me a manual he had written, which I subsequently read several times. Although it took years to find him again, his words nurtured my soul with good effect.

He wrote, "If you would hope for a life of wholeness, you've got to learn how to bring three elements of your life into balance." His first point is that everyone needs times of *solitude*. "You grievously wound yourself and others," he said, "when you don't take time to be by yourself." The people he had worked with who had the most difficult problems were people who did not spend enough time with themselves to know who they were and what they truly wanted. As a result, it was almost impossible to conduct meaningful transactions with others or even with God.

In short, my counselor acquaintance affirmed the need to withdraw to a place and time of solitude. One of my friends describes this process as nurturing his introversion. Another describes it as going into "the cave." Nehemiah 5:7 describes how Nehemiah stepped away from circumstances and "pondered them in my mind" (NIV) or "consulted with himself" (NASB).

One of Jesus' terms was "inner room" or "inner chamber," as in Matthew 6:6—"But you, when you pray, go into your inner room, and when you have shut your door, pray to your Father who is in secret, and your Father who sees in secret will repay you" (NASB). Whatever term you use, you must regularly turn off the music, the computer, and even people so you can get away to a deserted place. After you've been there, the God who sees in secret will reward you openly in His time.

God wants one-on-one time with you. You can talk with Him anytime, anywhere, but sometimes you won't have *meaningful* communication with God unless you've had enough one-on-one time with *yourself* to know what you need to talk about.

In my own spiritual growth I was at times so tied up in knots that I had to say, "I need time with me so that I can get ready to pray." Once I took a whole day out for a prayer retreat. I got there at 9:00 in the morning, but it was 2:00 before I was able to complete an entire sentence of focused prayer. I spent most of those first five hours pacing the floor, trying to get the noise in my head quiet enough that I could talk over it. I had been so busy with "things" that I was unable to think about God. I was like Martha, so consumed with dishes needing attention that I couldn't settle in for you-and-me time with God.

The psalmist said, "Be still and know that I am God." Until we get quiet enough, we can't hear what God is trying to say.

The prophet Elijah was a leading personality of his day. After three years of "alone" time with God by the brook Kerith (see 1 Kings 17:1-7), he could stand on a hillside before thousands of people, many of whom opposed him, and offer a prayer a half minute long. In answer, fire came down from heaven and consumed an altar (see 1 Kings 18:19-39). Thousands of people responded. Yet he became so discouraged that he wanted God to take his life (see 1 Kings 19:4).

What was God's solution? He led Elijah into a cave. After all the noise died down, he hears this little whisper that said, in effect, "I'm only beginning to show my strength. The work ahead of you will require three more people besides you. Go out and anoint two more kings and a successor for yourself" (see 1 Kings 19:15-17). We later read that Baal worship was effectively halted during the office of these people (see 2 Kings 10:28).

Several years ago Bill Hybels, pastor of North America's biggest church, came out with a book titled, *Too Busy Not to Pray*. He said most of us go through life so fast that we're revving our engines at 10,000 rpm's that were designed for only 5,000 rpm's. He said he had to create a journaling ritual that would help him slow down to the point where he could hear God. For him, he needed to cut back to the spiritual equivalent of 500 rpm's!

It takes time to get quiet! Can you get up earlier? Can you skip one meal a day or week? Can you give up some television? Most people could find 30 extra minutes a day to make space for quiet and solitude.

Do you want to have power in your small group? Check your solitude level. Do you know what to ask God for? Have you asked God to make you a blessing or to bless the people in your group? Is the life of intercession adequate for your group? If it's not in place, how do you expect to have divine interventions in your life and ministry?

There can be mental health consequences when the secret life is ignored. My counselor friend summarized his findings about people he had treated for various disorders that stemmed from being broken from reality. He said most could be traced to not having wholeness at the area of knowing who they are or what they wanted out of life. They had become separated and divided, with huge conflicts internally. To help them restore a sense of wholeness, he had to teach them to how to take time for themselves and for God.

The practice of helping someone else develop a life with God is now increasingly being called "spiritual direction." Many North American Christians do not recognize this term, because spiritual direction is not part of recent evangelical tradition. However, it seems to have been part of the church in the first few centuries. It formed the basis for the monastic movements of the Russian Orthodox and the orders of the Roman Catholic Churches. Through the centuries, Christians who had a need for deepening their life with God have found that other Christians can be a help as they talk the process over with them.

Jesus' command to ask, seek, and knock (see Matthew 7:7-8 and Luke 11:9-10) seems to be teaching, "If you want to look at a principle of the kingdom, learn to ask, seek, and knock." If you don't have any sense of yourself, you don't know how to compose a question for asking. You don't know what you're seeking. So even if you found it, you wouldn't recognize it. You don't know how to take the initiatives necessary to get doors opened by knocking. You will be more effective at each of these initiatives as you learn the discipline of solitude.

You Can Also Seek God through Community

Christians also need an experience of *community* with other people. Because of the brokenness of modern society, many men and women lack direct connection to the kind of community where they can find the help and resources they need. The counselor I described above offered this prescription for churches: staff members should invest themselves in equipping volunteers who can conduct small listening groups. These gatherings, in turn, can become communities where people will find wholeness in mental health and support for their journey.

How to Seek #3: Be part of a small-group community.

179

Staff members should invest themselves in equipping volunteers who can conduct small listening groups.

Wow! Here's someone in the mental health field who says "If there's a future for a person's wholeness, it will be found in communities of support." It was obvious to him that in our generation there's a profound loss of confidence in institutions. The police, government, schools, and other societal organizations have by and large lost their power to compel good behavior. Even the public school system has lost the confidence of many parents.

As you look around there is one institution on earth that has been charged with making God real to people. It is a Christian community, a church based on cells. Intimate ministry in such small groups is able to help people be whole.

Dr. Eddie Gibbs' book, *In Name Only*, talks about how people fall into nominalism—when they identify themselves as Christians, but lack a vital faith, an ongoing maturity in Christ, and a transformed lifestyle. He says the best preventer of nominalism is for Christians to be part of a small community of witness. Gibbs' book describes a living, vibrant community of witness that's able to demonstrate faith to people hungry for it, as well as to support those who are already disciples of Jesus.

Hot coals in a fireplace glow longer and brighter together than separately. A healthy small group will help prepare you for those times when you need to seek God in private.

Hot coals in a fireplace glow longer and brighter together than separately.

How to Seek #4:
Maintain a lifestyle characterized by simplicity.

Beware Lest Possessions Distract You

The third discipline is *simplicity*. People who are consumed with "things" can never be whole. Idolatry is closely related to love of money and love of possessions. As a result, you do not get freedom from things until you're ready to get rid of them. As long as you're trusting in things, you serve a God who is too small to be able to take your devotional intentions and translate them into blessings to others.

People who are consumed with "things" can never be whole.

Most of us are encumbered with many distractions. Most of us need to place a long-overdue phone call to the Salvation Army or Goodwill to reduce the amount of possessions that clutter our lives. Most Christians in North America can simplify their lives on several fronts: both extraneous obligations and unneeded property.

God sometimes sends the blessing of fires or earthquakes or stock market slumps to help us get rid of the same burdens and impediments that kept the rich young ruler from following Jesus. He sorrowed because he had great wealth (see Mark 10:17-23). We never heard if he made it into the kingdom of God. We saw him go away from following Christ with a heavy heart.

Doing the will of God must be the central preoccupation of the Christian. As Jesus promised, if we seek first the kingdom of God and His righteousness then He will provide for our needs, including food, clothing, and shelter (see Matthew 6:33).

Thus if anything you own prevents you from finding and doing the will of God, that thing is not worth owning. Less is more when you have divorced yourself of the cares of this world through simplicity.

You don't own things; they own you.

Someone once said, "You don't own things; they own you." When I come before the Lord and pray, "I want to be a real blessing to others," I don't want the Spirit to have to nudge me with the message, "Then get rid of this area because it's preventing you from being available to what I want to bless in your life." It is important to ask myself continually, "What can I give away or dispose of? I want to have a heart pure before God, not in conflict, not pulled and torn every which way." Simplicity requires making the good choices that will be nudged by the

Spirit of God as you pray, read the Word, talk to godly Christians, and look for ways to be a blessing to others.

The Christ Life Is a Walk by Faith

The Gospels contain some 200 references to people putting their faith, belief, or trust in Jesus. All three words come from the same root idea. Jesus regularly speaks of increasing in faith, He praises some people for great faith, and he faults others for lack of faith. In speaking of His second coming He asks, "When the Son of Man comes, will he find faith on the earth?" (Luke 18:8).

How to Seek #5: Exercise faith.

The Bible also links faith to seeking God: "And without faith it is impossible to please God, because anyone who comes to him must believe that he exists and that he rewards those who earnestly seek him" (Hebrews 11:6). Seeking God is an adventure that offers no resting point. You never reach a spot where you can coast in your relationship with Him.

Your effectiveness as a group leader will be in direct proportion to your willingness to grow and mature in Christ. The more Christ radiates through you, the more fully committed disciples will be formed through the group you lead.

How can the church here in North America speak in such a way that today's pluralistic generation will hear? Today's secular mindset is one characterized by many ideas but no standard for truth. The Christian, as an apostle or missionary of Jesus Christ, carries a life-changing message. How can it be heard?

One answer relates to credibility: Do Christians walk their talk? Actually, that criteria is only a beginning point. Communication in the rising generation will go far beyond walking our talk. The standard of integrity for the future will be much higher: Christians should not talk until they walk.

People's walk with Christ will be so genuine that when they talk, others will comment, "I *thought* you must be a Christian; now I understand." Evangelism and discipleship will be done on the basis of relationships. The church of tomorrow will look like a disciple-making church in direct relation to the integrity of our relationships.

182

Evangelism and discipleship will be done on the basis of relationships.

How will the church of the future become a place where we talk our walk? We start in the quiet place with God and then we bring people into our lives. Because they're taken into our lives, God brings them into His life—into His body.

A relational approach to evangelism invites people into loving fellowship saying, "We love you, we'll take you, we'll talk with you, we'll help you, we'll pray for you, we'll encourage you — and how are you with Jesus now?" As we love and accept people, they will come closer and closer to Christ. The distance will narrow much more rapidly within that level of fellowship than if these same people were left out of our company until they learn all the appropriate shibboleths of the Christian faith.

We are to do more than preach the gospel alone; our task is to offer the Body of Christ to our generation. It's not just a sermon we preach; it's a community we open. We have misdefined the gospel as being limited to a series of verbal propositions to be believed and taught. The really good news is that God invites you to join the Body of Jesus Christ, that the Holy Spirit will mark you as that body, and that you are invited to join a heavenly covenant group that will start on this earth and never end.

It's not just a sermon we preach; it's a community we open.

We've got to do more than pass on a message; we must offer a community that says: "God accepts you and here is a people who receive you as God does." Jesus will enter their lives because they become aware of Him while among you and me.

Are you ready to be used like that? If so, those around you will soon be in on your secret!

3

INTRODUCTION TO PART 3

D ON'T STOP READING YET! THE REMAINING PAGES WILL GIVE you added perspective on your pastor and on the role you can play. The book's final words will invite you to make a vital commitment certain to help speed you on your journey.

CHAPTER

13

YOUR PASTOR NEEDS YOUR HELP

WHERE DOES YOUR PASTOR FIT IN THIS IDEA OF LAY MOBILI-zation? Most pastors are trained to operate on the lone shepherd model. It's a modern version of Jesus' story about a herdsman who gathers 99 of his sheep, but finds that one is still outside. So he personally leaves the 99 to go and look for it (see Matthew 18:12-14, Luke 15:4-7).

In applying that model, today's clergy head out to the home, hospital, courtroom, juvenile detention hall, unemployment office, and anywhere else members of their flock may be in crisis. Propelled by noble motives and genuine concern, these pastors desire to minister to each sheep in need. As the number of sheep who are lost or in trouble increases, many clergy are hard pressed to keep pace.

Their first obstacle is huge spans of care—huge numbers of people for which to care. Today's clergy-to-people ratio ranges from 1:75 to 1:250, depending on denomination and other factors. Even a church with average worship attendance of 75 or fewer people (some 50% of North American churches) generally represents a total flock of well over a hundred when you take into account fringe members, lapsed

187

members, occasional attenders, and recent visitors.

A second and bigger obstacle to the lone shepherd model is that few churches exist today where 99 people are healthy and only one is wandering or in trouble. Dysfunctionality certainly runs higher than 1% in the typical church (the percentage will depend on how tightly the word is defined). Broken homes, victims of physical or sexual abuse, addictions, and serious medical illness all have a traumatizing effect on people and therefore increase their neediness.

Neediness may be reaching its highest level ever in the history of the United States, with mobility and corporate restructuring producing changes like those seen after the Civil War or during the 1930's and 1940's as the Great Depression took its toll. One important indicator today is that one half of pre-college children are being raised by their biological parents. In other words, half of today's children will spend at least part of their childhood cut off from one or both of their natural parents. Thus the rate of blended families, step-parenting, and single parenting is at a very high level. The social dislocations and potentials for abuse are terrifying.

Neediness may be reaching its highest level ever in the history of the United States.

Gone are the days when a pastor could merely kiss babies; preside over baptisms, funerals, and weddings; orchestrate Sabbath rituals for the congregation at worship; and then have the leisure to ask, "Who else can I help?" Faithful ministers have always put in long hours of sacrificial service. Yet there was usually a dimension of fundamental primary care they could assume was in place because "Mom" and sometimes "Dad" were responsible for it.

That family-based society no longer exists to the same extent it once did. North American culture today doesn't place the same values on the nurturing role that "Mom" (or "Dad") played in yesteryear. "Aunt," "Uncle," "Grandma," "Grandpa," and "Cousin" often no longer live nearby to create a sense of shared parenting or extended family. Judeo-Christian standards of right and wrong do not flavor a community the same way they used to. In fact, large numbers of people don't even have an identity with our geographical community; the vast majority of us are located within huge, impersonal metropolitan areas incapable of noticing or responding if our lives fall apart.

The net result is that a lot of raw needs and pain go untreated. Dislocation, loss of job security, economic turmoil and convulsions, and other transitions compound these dilemmas. Tune in to a radio talk show for five minutes or conduct a brief interview with a social worker or school counselor. You'll become convinced that ordinary people today are struggling with unprecedented levels of personal issues. You'll also be reminded that in their search for answers, they often have no one present to bring them the love of Christ.

The net result is that a lot of raw needs and pain go untreated.

A third difficulty with the lone shepherd model is that today's trends offer little sign of letup. Society is making people sick faster than churches are making them well. The neediness of people is all around.

A fourth difficulty of the lone shepherd model is that it disenfranchises the laity from their God-given ministries, thus denying them the fullness of their Christian birthright!

Society is making people sick faster than churches are making them well.

The Only Long-Term Solution

Let me be clear: I'm not writing to criticize your pastor. Today's clergy, if statistically described, have more formal training, better sermon preparation tools, better support resources, and more counseling skills than of any generation to date. Except for certain hucksters whose greed or moral scandals are splashed across the news media, the vast majority of pastors today genuinely desire to care for needy sheep in Jesus' name. They also want to find a pathway toward greater effectiveness in doing so.

Will a solution come if you or they bring an additional minister on staff? Usually not. How many people would your church have to hire if paid helpers were the only ones allowed to meet all the needs screaming for care? Not even the best-endowed churches on this continent have enough financial resources to cover *all* the empty bases.

If your church is going to be effective in the future, it faces some major decisions. It cannot be content with business as usual. When you see the problem of society falling apart and the foundations of social order unraveling, is there a way to deal forthrightly with it? As the Psalmist lamented, "If the foundations be destroyed, what can the righteous do?" (Psalm 11:3, ASV). Perhaps one answer is to rebuild them. Groups can be one of the "new" foundational elements for social order.

> **"If the foundations be destroyed, what can the righteous do?" ...Perhaps one answer is to rebuild them.**

The Most Important Thing You Can Do

Who, then, is responsible today for the care of souls? Clergy never had to carry that charge alone. Families were somewhat more stable in previous generations. Although they certainly had problems, they often had support from relatives living in the area. They got by with fewer helpers outside of the family.

Families today need spiritual nurturers who take somewhat of a parent role. The job is too big to be limited to professionals. There are simply not enough paid pastors to go around for them to be the primary or only caregivers.

We must empower a new class of Christian worker (which is really a return to the New Testament model). This person is called a lay minister, volunteer leader, Sunday school class care coordinator, small group leader, and the like. We've got to empower these servants of Christ not simply to teach, but to offer pastoral care.

We must empower a new class of Christian worker ...to offer pastoral care.

What the typical person today needs is a shoulder to cry on, an ear for listening, some wise counsel, and appropriate personal account-ability. We need a far more invasive and intimate resource of support than we've previously experienced outside the family. Otherwise our social foundations might crumble further, resulting in even more moral anarchy.

This book is designed to help you decentralize the ministry of your church to the level of small, spiritual families. Cells, as a unit of society, did tremendous good in Wesley's England of the 18th century. They also transformed post-war Korea in Seoul. They are currently bringing social stability to many regions of Africa, contributing to that continent's development as the fastest-growing segment of Christendom in the world.

Here's but one example. Two hundred years ago, John Wesley and his followers blanketed the country with their revivalist preaching. Then these itinerant ministers would organize people into small groups, called class meetings. Trained leaders asked pointed questions like, "What temptations did you meet this week and how did you deal with them?" After being that frank with each other, they then could pursue holiness with integrity, they would pray together, see victories, pull their families together, and make a difference. For decades Methodists were "the" Christian denomination that helped people get their lives together.

What kind of leadership does your church need to foster in order to develop that level of community building? It doesn't occur in large gatherings of hundreds nearly as well as in small meetings of a dozen or less. Actually, the best community building that researchers can find takes place in groups of 10 or so. Most of the issues that people need support for can be handled in a small spiritual kinship group. The main human ingredient is a leader willing to pull 5 to 15 people together, see that they are loved and nurtured, orchestrate some form of Bible study with them, and help them use their spiritual gifts both in and out of the group to touch lives in service to Christ.

Volunteer leaders can fill that role quite well. They can often do it better than pastoral staff members because they can remain concentrated on those 10 or so people, giving them the ongoing prayer, support, guidance, and encouragement they need. They can give care to a few consistently rather than only in crises.

The game plan for the future is simple. The volunteer leader works with the 10, and the church staff sees to it that these lay leaders receive the necessary training and resources. The church staff can also take the toughest cases and work with them on the side. In that way, a huge number of people receive care without proportionately expanding the budget of the church.

The game plan for the future is simple. The volunteer leader works with the 10, and the church staff sees to it that these lay leaders receive the necessary training and resources.

Will You Join the Revolution?

The jury is no longer out for North America. Wherever people are engaged in being cared for in cells, their reports of satisfaction are heart warming. The stories that come out of such groups are beyond what people typically hope or pray for. Amazing quality-of-care levels are emerging in church after church that decentralizes or "gives away" the ministry into smaller, caring units.

It really doesn't matter what you name the caring units. Label them as ministry teams, committees, task forces, boards, cell groups, Bible studies, or Sunday schools. The key isn't what you call them. The important factor is that empowered lay ministers are taking responsibility for promoting the spiritual well-being and care of other people.

In such groups, the Holy Spirit shows up, just as promised. In effect, Jesus has said that He will attend a cell group's meetings or the one-on-one encounters outside the scheduled gathering time. That divine pledge (see Matthew 18:20) makes a difference.

One characteristic of the New Testament church that sometimes we don't see today is how the believers experienced a spiritual community in which the truth was spoken and love was experienced. Love was their credential of being Jesus' disciples, making truth irresistible (see John 13:34-35, Ephesians 4:15, 1 Peter 1:22). Truth and love are best given and received in a small group.

Love was their credential of being Jesus' disciples, making truth irresistible.

People heard truth from people who loved them. If the goal was telling the truth, then the context was one in which the hearers sensed that they were loved and therefore they listened.

People today, as in all times, are hurting for a lack of love. Will you lead your group to establish new standards of caregiving and truth telling? Will you explore what may be new ways of raising up additional disciplemakers in the process? If you accept this invitation, you will partner in a change that gives a new face to the church in North America.

CHAPTER

14

READ THIS ONLY IF YOU'RE A PASTOR OR CHURCH STAFF MEMBER

T HIS BOOK IS DESIGNED PRIMARILY FOR A CHURCH'S "VOLUN-
teer" force, with the clergy cheering them on. The few pages in
this chapter are the only ones written specifically for pastors,
ministry staff, and other church professionals.

During my 16 years of pastoring, I watched many people become
Christians through lay-led small groups. In a number of cases I saw a
more successful discipleship regimen than occurred among even the
most devoted students of my preaching! I also saw the power of
leadership development through small groups. I became amazed at how
durable small groups can be. I constantly marveled how well they met
people's needs.

As hard as I tried, I couldn't figure out why the small cell was often
more effective in care and discipleship than the large celebration-size
gathering. The best I could do was to lift up my perplexities in prayer:
"Lord, something very right is happening in these small units. Help me
to see what You are doing."

It was not until years later that I better understood the dynamics
involved. In 1978, through a series of divinely orchestrated confirma-

tions, I left local church ministry to become a church consultant. In 1984, after six years of analyzing churches and learning from other researchers, the Lord began to bring the clarity for which I had prayed. My colleagues and I began earnest examination of the concepts God was revealing. We visited and conducted interviews with the role models He was raising up around the world.

Then in 1988 we began inviting teams of pastors and their staffs to review our findings. Their reaction was consistently enthusiastic: "You have to share this stuff with others." So we began a series of invitation-only conferences designed to teach, piece by piece, what we had been exploring in "laboratory" settings.

No one knew whether these ideas about small-group care, evangelism, and leadership development would cause unexpected side effects or other unintended consequences! Over several years of testing, we gradually accumulated experience in churches large and small, established and new, growing and declining, denominational and independent, suburban and center city, mono-cultural and multi-ethnic. Through this experimentation we were able to identify which patterns fit across the board.

By working with churches of all sizes, in all parts of the continent, and in all major denominations and worship traditions, I have become convinced that God is leading many churches in a quiet revolution. This transformation or change is significant because it is allowing Spirit-filled, God-gifted people to focus on loving one another, speaking the truth in love, and releasing additional leaders who can multiply the reformation elsewhere. The consequences are that many, many people are being provoked to love and good works through healthy, reproducing small groups. To a certain extent, even the foundations of our society are being rebuilt through this lay-driven movement.

I have become convinced that God is leading many churches in a quiet revolution.

The book, *Prepare Your Church for the Future,* presents the grand theory of these transferable practices. A later book, *The Coming*

Church Revolution: Empowering Leaders for the Future, shows more than 40 specific examples of how the theory works. A number of additional resources, including audiotapes, videotapes, and structured mentoring manuals, train church leaders in how to apply and coach others in these perspectives.

Thus my work up to this point had been addressed primarily to pastors, although a surprising number of eager elders, board members, and group leaders have followed these writings and training as well.

The book you are now reading addresses, "How do the people of the church prepare to take part in this revolution?"

That question raises a more fundamental issue: *Why* mobilize the laity? Often a pastor's initial motive is to offload the great pressure felt from being surrounded by people in need. As intense as those pressures can be, is the need to spread around the pastor's work an adequate enough reason for mobilizing the laity?

The previous pages presuppose an even broader rationale. Gift-based, body-wide mobilization through small groups leads people to be in communion with each other at an accountability level. An empowered and released people will create classes, cells, groups, teams, task forces, committees, and boards designed to care for one another's souls, along with whatever stated purpose their group has. This renewed sense of lay-led body life can rebuild the very foundations of social order. The restoration of fundamental community represents the greatest ministry opportunity and challenge of our lifetime.

The restoration of fundamental community represents the greatest ministry opportunity and challenge of our lifetime.

How can you as a professional best cooperate with God in changing the ministry culture of the church you serve? You can do so by prayerfully and repeatedly examining the ministry practices of those volunteers who lead small groups. Through modeling and coaching, you can guide your people into new paradigms and practices.

Using the principles highlighted in this book, you are perhaps 37 months away from a permanent culture change in the ministry practices of your congregation. Why? Your congregation needs three year-long cycles to develop the role models, track records, and new traditions, while also overcoming the "we've always done it that way" habits and perspectives that sometimes hinder different ways of approaching ministry. By the time you enter your fourth year of transition—the 37th month— these lay-empowered practices will have taken root. The result will be a church that reaches, assimilates, and cares for an ever-enlarging harvest field.

How can such a broad reality be examined and changed by looking closely at only one part of church life? Because it's such a foundational component. Virtually all ministry in most churches occurs through sub-units of the whole congregation.

You are perhaps 37 months away from a permanent culture change in the ministry practices of your congregation.

What a wonderful future to foresee as volunteer ministers care for people and then bring them together for corporate worship.

15

CHAPTER

CONCLUSION

BILL HYBELS IS SENIOR PASTOR OF THE CHURCH THAT CURRENT-
ly has more recognized small groups than any other congregation
in North America. He and his staff regularly gather all small-
group leaders for special times of vision, skill training, and peer-level
huddling.

At one of those meetings, Pastor Hybels pointed out that the idea of
shepherding people for Jesus ties into a central theme of Scripture. He
observed that Psalm 23, perhaps the best-loved passage in the Old
Testament, affirms that "God, as shepherd, is watching over us." A
thousand years later Jesus personalized this concept by saying, "*I* am
the good shepherd" (John 10:11, italics added). In some of Jesus' last
words on earth, He commanded Peter to make sure the shepherding
continues: "Feed my sheep," Jesus said three times (John 21:15-17).
Then Peter in turn enlisted local church elders in the process. "You've
got some shepherding to do as an example for the rest of the congregation," Peter said in effect in 1 Peter 5:2-5.

I invite each reader to make an ongoing commitment to expand your
role in God's shepherding agenda. As the title of this book implies, *Nine
Keys to Effective Small Group Leadership,* you have nine choices
before you, each of which will move you in the direction of greater

effectiveness in your service to Christ. Will you prayerfully register a faith promise to God by checking the appropriate boxes below? Then will you invite someone else to witness what you've done and to hold you accountable to that pledge?

My readiness and intentions in my role as

☐ Small group leader ☐ Apprentice leader ☐ Future apprentice or group leader

(Please place a ✓ for all that apply)

☐	1. CONNECT	I will be available for debriefing interviews with the church staff.
☐	2. RECRUIT	I will recruit my replacement(s) before we begin meeting with the group, and I will help my replacement(s) develop an ability to lead.
☐	3. INVITE	I will reach out between meetings, cultivating both old and new contacts.
☐	4. PREPARE	I will prepare my mind and heart for our meetings and will include my apprentice(s) in the process.
☐	5. MEET	I will conduct meetings that encourage believers and accept seekers.
☐	6. BRING	I will bring group members to worship for the church's weekend services.
☐	7. SERVE	I will serve others with my gifts, knowledge, energy, time, and money, conscious that my greatest influence may occur as I set an example.
☐	8. WIN	I will make time to build acquaintances with unbelievers, serving them at their points of struggle.
☐	9. SEEK	I will meet regularly with God in private prayer.

_____   _____

signed (yourself)   date

_____   _____

signed (witness)   date

Permission is given to reproduce this page for use in small-group settings and training events.

Sooner or later, healthy cells led by prayerful people replicating through apprentice leaders are going to see two to four converts per year each. They will also see new cells birth. They will make more and better disciples than is possible in most large-group contexts. When these things happen, we will see an entire population impacted for Jesus Christ.

This entire book boils down to four universal principles which, if applied, could be foundational to a church taking a greater part in God's redemption of humanity: (1) Learn how to listen to God when you pray—Key Nine of this book, (2) bring newcomers to faith—Keys Eight and Seven, (3) care for others—Keys Six, Five, Four, and Three, (4) and replicate yourself by multiplying leaders through the church Keys Two and One. None of these vital practices will ever become obsolete.

You and I have abundant testimony to the fact that Jesus Christ is still on Earth. His Holy Spirit is still drawing people to himself. Wherever two or three gather in His name, He shows up in a special way. Further, there is a willingness evident on the part of clergy of all denominations to share their care load with the people of the church.

We have been given the privilege of being shepherds under Jesus Christ through the role of leader in a small group. What better environment in which to bring a new convert or a seeker? What better environment than a small group into which to pour energy, time, and love? And what more likely environment to experience durable life-change as you experience God in ways "immeasurably more than all we ask or imagine, according to his power that is at work within us" (Ephesians 3:20).

May God bless you richly in your journey!

APPENDICES

For Those Who Have Read
Other "Carl George" Titles

THE PATH TO MATURITY OFTEN INVOLVES REVISITING PLACES that have been significant influences in our journey. Often we see these valuable "stones of remembrance" with new insight.

Sometimes these are literal rocks. I remember a well-used afternoon where I spent an extended prayer time while sitting on a boulder in the mountains of southern California. At the time I was fearful about the loss of financial and emotional support that was certain to accompany a step of faith I was about to take. Where does God's peace come from at times like those? I read clearly that God will be my portion: "You are my portion, O Lord; I have promised to obey your words" (Psalm 119:57; see also Psalm 142:5; 73:26).

He promised to be all I needed; to *be* the portion, not just *provide* it. "If you're the portion, that's all that's needed forever," I was able to say. That promise gave me the freedom to leave our family's current support system and to throw ourselves onto God.

Sometimes the rocks we revisit are memories of teaching points and significant breakthroughs God gave us, based on truths from His Word. For those who have journeyed with me over the years as I have learned, the following list represents the "top sites" I've revisited in recent months and gained the most new perspective. These concepts represent the intuitive concepts I had to surrender and the "counter-intuitive" discoveries I had to embrace in order to make ongoing progress in my journey forward:

1. **Decentralized caregiving:** People today desperately need care, and the missing operative is not additional clergy, so much as a system of lay pastoring that focuses on mutual "one another" ministry. The key to having more people receive care is to increase the number of volunteer spiritual caregivers.

Common wisdom: Training should focus on increasing the clergy's caregiving.

New discovery: Laypeople must be developed as spiritual caregivers.

2. **Community-assisted life change**: Christians change in the context of a small group more readily and more durably than they do on their own.

Common wisdom: "Anointed" preaching effectively urges people to make life changes.

New discovery: Small-group settings invite durable community-assisted life change.

3. **"Overcrowding" is a red herring:** The primary obstacle to a healthy network of groups is not a lack of available classroom space, so much as a lack of trained, available leaders who are receiving ongoing coaching for ministry.

Common wisdom: New groups won't form when classroom space is maximized out.

New discovery: Coached leaders will generate new groups and discover new venues.

4. **Frequently unrealized group potential:** There is tremendous life potential in every meeting. The announced purpose of why the group meets is almost beside the point. The generic concept of a group helps you dig out that reality. All small groups are comprised of four generic qualities which vary in percentage: loving, learning, tasking, and maintaining. The encouragement factor or "heart" is what gives a group its greatest vitality.

Common wisdom: Some groups contribute to community building; others don't.

New discovery: Any group can build "community" through increased nurture.

5. **Newcomer survival principle:** When people's first exposure to a

church is accompanied by a small-group relationship, they are far more likely to be part of that church six months later. Why? Breaking in is easier with an accomplice or sponsor.

Common wisdom: To build worship attendance, keep attracting new visitors.

New discovery: Relationships are the main reason a person visits or returns.

6. **Group-driven worship services**: Congregations are really aggregations of small groups. Thus you can build attendance by assembling subunits. The more strongly people are connected by relationship, the more likely they are to journey together to a service of divine worship—whether the service is exciting or not!

Common wisdom: Platform talent in worship leads to word-of-mouth excitement.

New discovery: Small-group networks encourage relationally supported worship participation.

7. **Affinity attraction factor**: People pre-select each other based on relationships of affinity, as illustrated by the puppy principle.

Common wisdom: Assignment-based care (A-Z or ZIP codes) prevents people from being overlooked.

New discovery: People accept care best if you honor interpersonal "chemistry."

8. **Mystery of the re-appearing open chair**: There is a simple explanation behind the mystery of how newcomers come into closed groups: group members classify friends differently than they do unknown strangers. Even closed groups welcome already-accepted "friends." Open chairs in small groups may be both visible and invisible.

Common wisdom: The best way to open a closed group is to mandate it.

New discovery: A group doesn't have to declare itself open to be open.

9. **Focal point for discipleship**: Discipleship occurs more in the leadership nucleus than in the group as a whole.

Common wisdom: All group members should receive similar discipleship help.

New discovery: Rising leaders need special attention in discipleship.

10. **Role Transition**: Leaders train their successors from the most basic roles to the most complex ones. By learning new perspectives on the many roles they play, leaders can identify the next area in which they should replace themselves.

Common wisdom: The more people you can touch, the more effective you are.

New discovery: Ministry multiplies best through 4 to 10 key relationships.

11. **Leadership "fertility" levels and lead times**: A group's growth rate and multiplication is best predicted by the number and role of apprentices. The apprentice factor is far more strategic than the age of the group, size of the group, or the amount of training the leadership nucleus has received.

Common wisdom: A group should divide when it reaches a certain size or age.

New discovery: A group multiplies naturally when the leadership transitions from apprentice to leader.

12. **Splash-free change**: Church people cooperate with culture change best when they are allowed to sample or copy an existing success, rather than by reacting and resisting a top-down announcement of "what we're going to do."

Common wisdom: Make churchwide announcement as soon as plan is decided.

New discovery: Do coaching and apprentice development; then brag on the results.

APPENDIX

B

FIND X SURVEY

Find X Survey

The purpose of this survey is to enable the church staff to become acquainted with you and your background, and to expand our congregation's small group ministry. Please circle or fill in your answers, as appropriate.

When were you born? (Month, Year) [/   ]

Approximately when did you begin attending here?
          (Month, Year) [/   ]

Please tell us about yourself. Circle as many as apply:

Male	Parent with children at home
Female	Parent with grown children
Married	Head of household
Single or single again	Widow or widower
Other_____	

Before coming here, did you regularly attend another church?
          Yes   No
  If no, what was your situation before starting to come here?
          Living out of this area
          Occasionally attending another church in this area
          Not attending any church
          Other_____

What is your denominational background?_____

_____

If you hold a leadership role or office in this church, please specify:

_____

_____

If you presently take part in a class or group sponsored by our church, please specify:

_____

_____

Have you ever served as a Church School, Sunday School, or Home Bible Class leader or teacher (or similar)?

        Yes   No

Have you ever served as a Scout Leader, Sports Coach, Club Sponsor, or in any other role as a group organizer or leader?

        Yes   No

Do you have experience in public speaking? If yes, please describe:

_____

_____

What is your occupation?

_____

If your occupation involves supervising others, please describe in what capacity:

_____

What involvement(s) are you willing to consider at this church? Circle as many as apply:

    Choose a home group to visit from a list of locations and meeting times.

    Have my name given as a prospect to small group leaders.

    Attend a mixer at which I could meet and select from among several small group leaders.

    Come to an overview briefing which explains what group leaders do.

    Open my home to be a place where a small group could meet.

    Assist someone in building a small group as an assistant.

Assist someone in building a small group as an apprentice.
Take a course in "how to lead a small group."
Lead a small group or class that I would develop from scratch.
Other_____

_____

Women, please respond to this question: Would you prefer (check as many as apply):

A group led by a woman	A daytime group
A group consisting of all women	An evening group
A mixed gender group	A weekend group
A couples' group	A specific-issue support group
A Bible study group	A prayer group

Other_____

Your name, if you wish a follow up contact:

_____

Your mailing address:

_____

Your evening telephone number, and best times to call:

_____

Your daytime telephone number, if okay to use for personal matters:

_____

Your fax number, if okay to use for personal matters:

_____

Your e-mail address, if okay to use for personal matters:

_____

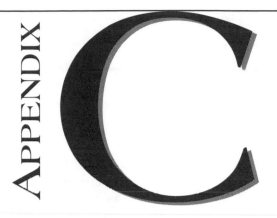

Annotated Listing of Spiritual Gifts Inventories

Houts Inventory of Spiritual Gifts

This brief questionnaire by Richard Houts draws from the Baptist tradition and tests for 16 spiritual gifts. No sign gifts are tested. It includes a unique section detailing opportunities for ministry gift use within the Body of Christ.

Discover Your Gifts Series

The three volumes, all by Don and Katie Fortune, are titled *Discover Your God-Given Gifts, Discover Your Spouse's Gifts,* and *Discover Your Children's Gifts*. Each is more than 200 pages long and contains substantial general teaching on spiritual gifts. Through more than two decades of marriage counseling, this husband-and-wife team have created numerous Scripture-filled assessment tools which are included in these books. The Fortunes believe the Bible describes three kinds of gifts: manifestation (1 Corinthians 12), ministry (Ephesians 4), and motivational (Romans 12 and 1 Peter 4).

Mobilizing Spiritual Gifts Series

Paul Ford created the *Mobilizing Spiritual Gifts* series to help a local church or ministry establish a wholistic way to release lay persons into service through a discovery and mobilization process. Key components include a Biblical curriculum, six assessment tools, an interview process, placement enhanced by accurate lay ministry job descriptions, and follow-up monitoring. Two curriculum versions are offered: one that encourages the "sign" gifts and one that does not.

Network

Network, pioneered and tested through Willow Creek Community Church, helps believers identify their God-given passion, spiritual gifts, and personal style. It provides both a volunteer identification and a placement process. The accompanying tools includes videos, Bible exploration, and a one-on-one consultation. The *Participant's Manual* tests for 23 spiritual gifts, including sign gifts, craftsmanship, counseling, and creative communication.

Spiritual Gifts Inventory

More than 1.6 million copies are in circulation of this 108-question, self-assessment inventory by Larry Gilbert. It can be completed and evaluated in about 20 minutes. A more comprehensive kit, called Team Ministry, is designed to organize the whole congregation according to spiritual gifts. The kit includes the inventory as well as an implementation manual, a teacher's manual, a textbook, planning materials, audiocassettes, and the inventory itself.

Spiritual Gifts Self-Discovery

This 125-question survey of 25 different spiritual gifts created by Robert D. Noble is especially popular in mainline churches. Supplemental materials introduce the idea of spiritual gifts, offer a Biblical framework for understanding them, and show how a church can be more intentional about developing and focusing gifts for use in its parish.

Wagner-Modified Houts

This questionnaire, with over a million copies in print, tests for 25 spiritual gifts. It covers the core lists summarized in Romans 12 and 1 Corinthians 12, including tongues, interpretation, and prophecy. It also discusses celibacy, exorcism, voluntary poverty, and discernment of spirits. The description of each gift contains a suggested definition and appropriate Scriptures.

Wesley Spiritual Gifts Questionnaire

Modeled after the Wagner-Modified Houts Questionnaire, this analysis defines 24 gifts from a Wesleyan point of view. It includes gifting categories for craftsmanship (artistic and manual) and music (vocal and instrumental).

Any or all of the above titles can also be obtained from:

Kingdom Inc.
Attn.: Dept. NK
P.O. Box 486
Mansfield, PA 16933

Phone 1-800-597-1123
FAX (717) 662-3875
internet: http://www.kingdom.com

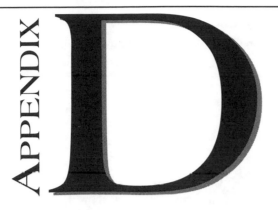

APPENDIX

RESOURCE MATERIALS
AUTHORED OR RECOMMENDED BY
CARL F. GEORGE

BOOKS

Leading and Managing the Local Church, by Carl F. George and Robert E.
    Logan

Prepare Your Church for the Future, by Carl F. George

How to Break Growth Barriers, by Carl F. George with Warren Bird

The Coming Church Revolution: Empowering Leaders for the Future, by
    Carl F. George with Warren Bird

*Nine Keys to Effective Small Group Leadership: How Lay Leaders Can
    Establish Dynamic and Healthy Cells, Classes or Teams,* by Carl
    F. George with Warren Bird

AUDIO LIBRARY SELF STUDY SERIES

Breaking the 200 Barrier

Beyond 400

Beyond 800

Lay Ministry: Training Leaders of a Care Group System (Meta-Church Green
    Zone)

Worship: Making Celebrations Come Alive (Meta-Church Red Zone)

Outreach: Building Bridges to Your Community (Meta-Church
    Yellow Zone)

How to Handle Conflict and Change

Nine Facets of the Effective Small Group Leader. Audio series with full
text of lectures and 1125 quiz items (These lectures are also
available in video. See below.)

<u>VIDEO SERIES</u>

Share the Vision (6 programs on 5 VHS cassettes)

Nine Facets of the Effective Small Group Leader. Nine VHS cassettes with
available Viewer's Guide. (These lectures also available in
audio with text of lectures and quiz items. See above.)

<u>EXTENDED TRAINING MODULE SERIES</u> (Guides for docents and
mentors)

#1 Coaching: Essential Skills for Leadership Development

#2 Telecare: Lay Ministry Care and Outreach

#3 Leadership: Recruiting and Training Volunteer Ministers

#4 Worship: Preparing More and Better Services

#5 Multiplying Churches: Planting New Congregations in and nearby
Existing Congregations, by Carl F. George and J.V. Thomas

<u>OTHER USEFUL TOOLS</u>

What Visitors See: A photographic project leading to discovering
improvements.

Planning Guides for Church Leaders: Workbooks for individual and
retreat use.

Problem Solving in the Church: Three step method for micro-planning
improvements. By David Luecke.

To contact the Author:

Carl F. George, Director
Center for the Development of Leadership for Ministry
P.O. Box 5407, Dept. 9K
Diamond Bar, CA 91765-5407
Voice Mail: 909-396-6843
FAX: 909-396-6845
Email: CarlGeorge@metachurch.com